ICONS

Classic
Rock
Covers

Classic Rock Covers

Michael Ochs

TASCHEN

KÖLN LONDON MADRID NEW YORK PARIS TOKYO

To Sandee With Love

Page/Seite 2:
Michael Ochs in the Michael Ochs Archives, Los Angeles, 1994
Photo: Jonathan Hyams

© 2001 TASCHEN GmbH
Hohenzollernring 53, D–50672 Köln
www.taschen.com

Text by Michael Ochs, Venice (CA), USA, 2001
Editorial coordination by Nina Schmidt, Cologne
Cover design by Angelika Taschen, Cologne
French translation by Patrick Javault, Paris
German translation by Ulrike Wasel, Klaus Timmermann, Düsseldorf

Printed in Italy
ISBN 3–8228–5540–5

Contents

Inhalt

Sommaire

6 Prelude

11 Präludium

17 Prélude

22 1950s

72 1960s

112 1970s

156 1980s–90s

189 Index

Prelude

When rock and roll and I were both very young, we started a friendship that, despite its ups and downs, has lasted all these years. When first introduced to rock in the early 50s, I decided that I had to learn everything about this new companion. My goal in life was to hear every rock record ever made. Now that my collection numbers well over 100,000 records, it gets increasingly diffcult to see the trees for the forest. When I agreed to do this book, I was looking forward to not only seeing the trees once again, but also to looking back at the roots of my record collecting mania.

The first records I remember seeing at home in the early 50s were my father's albums, namely Louis Armstrong, Louis Prima, Julie London and Doris Day. At the beginning of my teenage years, I wasn't hip enough to appreciate Prima and Armstrong, but the Day and London records definitely caught my eye, if not my ear. Actually, rock and roll did not introduce me to sex; the cleavage covers of the Day and London albums did.

My record buying began with rock and roll 45s since they only cost 89 cents, whereas albums were $3.98. On an allowance of 50 cents a week, purchasing records was not easy, so I soon turned to a life of crime. I made a box with a false bottom which I would take into the listening booth at my local record store. For every record they saw me take into the booth, three or four more would magically disappear into the box.

I must have successfully stolen hundreds of records before my hubris got me into trouble. I heard a new record called *Letter To An Angel* by the Five Shillings on the radio one week and knew I had to steal it from the store as soon as possible because it was too ethnic for continued airplay. The store was empty when I got there and in my head I knew that it was too dangerous, but my heart got the better of me. Sure enough I got caught. Eventually they let me go – after informing my parents of the crime. My father punished me but he also felt sorry for me and told me that when he was a kid and couldn't afford new records, he used to buy them used from jukebox companies.

The next weekend I raced downtown to check out all the jukebox companies I could find. Sure enough, they did sell used 45s for 25 cents each; however, I could still only afford two records a week. Then I found out that there was a terminally ill disc jockey in the hospital where my father worked. I went to visit him and asked if he'd be willing to do a radio show for the other patients through the hospital sound system. He said he'd love to if there were just some way to get the records. I told him I'd return next week with records.

I went back to the jukebox companies and got them to donate records for the hospital. I didn't get to keep the records, but I soon had hundreds of records a week passing through my house. As a teenager I didn't care about ownership: I just had to hear as much music as possible, and now I knew I could get 45s for free legally.

The first album I ever bought was the second Elvis Presley album, not because I didn't like the first one, but because I found the second one on sale at a hardware store for $1.98 rather than the standard price of $3.98. Getting my first album was very similar to getting my first girlfriend. Ah, the anticipation on the ride home. I stared at the beatic picture of Elvis on the cover, turned it over and read the liner notes, fondled the cover, peeked inside at the inner sleeve, looked at the vinyl, paused and then went back over every inch of the cover again. All that foreplay before I even got home to lay the record on the turntable was exquisite. Much to my surprise, it was all killer, no filler. Most rock albums I had heard at friends' houses contained just one or two hits and a lot of extraneous material. Soon I was collecting albums as well as singles.

For a number of reasons, albums seemed much more adult than singles. Albums were showcased on shelves and not kept in portable boxes. Albums expanded the aural experience with a visual. Albums were 5 inches bigger and 4 times more expensive. Finally, you could hold the album cover while listening to the music and the music played for almost 20 minutes before you had to change the record. No comparison: one was an affair while the other was a relationship.

The early covers were designed to capture teen America in all its innocence. Rock and roll was considered to be far too sexual for adult America at the time, so the album covers for the most part had to be one hundred per cent wholesome. Although most of the early rock artists were black, teenage America was a white world. So most of the record covers showed white teenagers in typical teen scenes. It's amazing how many black artists had pictures of white people on their record covers, while their own pictures were relegated to the back cover, if they were there at all.

Rock and roll came from blacks adding rhythm to the blues, but whites tried to usurp the music. Many black originals were covered by white artists such as Georgia Gibbs, Bill Haley, the McGuire Sisters and Pat Boone. Boone stole the hits from the black originals on *Ain't That A Shame, At My Front Door, I'll Be Home* and *I Almost Lost My Mind*. He and Little Richard both hit the charts with Richard's *Long Tall Sally*. Richard claimed Boone could never totally steal the song because he sang the words so fast that Boone would never be able to decipher the lyrics. Looking at the picture of the Little Richard album cover with his screaming, sweating face next to Boone's collegiate cover complete with white bucks, the teenager finally was confronted with the difference in vivid black and white, and black soon became his color of choice.

But just as rock and roll was hitting full stride, disaster struck. Little Richard saw God and gave up the devil's music, Elvis Presley got drafted and Buddy Holly and Eddie Cochran got killed in plane and car crashes respectively.

On top of that, the payola scandals killed Alan Freed's career. Freed had been one of the wildest disc jockeys in the country who put on the biggest and best rock concerts and even refused to play the white versions of the black hits. So, in the late 50s and early 60s, rock and roll was reduced to the safe sound of manufactured teen idols like Frankie Avalon, Fabian, Bobby Vee, Johnny Tillotson, Ricky Nelson and Bobby Rydell. Besides their wholesome pictures on the album covers, the liner notes also attested to the fact that these artists were not just rockers – they aspired to improve themselves beyond rock and roll by studying acting and dancing.

As rock and roll was dying prematurely in the U.S., the seeds that Bill Haley, Eddie Cochran and Gene Vincent had planted in England took root with British bands like The

Beatles, The Rolling Stones, The Animals, The Yardbirds and The Who. Then, as the 60s really took off, the roots of rock and roll started sprouting offshoots in every direction simultaneously. Folk-Rock, Surf, Soul, Psychedelia, Garage, Motown and the British invasion combined to make a rock revolution that was unstoppable. The music of teenage America was now the sound of a generation, and the generation was more grown up and global. At last the record covers could truly reflect the times. The cover of Steve Miller's first album could not be deciphered unless you were stoned. David Bowie appeared in a dress on the cover of his first album, and Jimi Hendrix could include a bevy of nude women on his album cover – at least in England.

When I left college, I gave all my records away except for a hundred of my favorites. A true hippie of the 60s, I swore that I would never own more possessions than I could fit in the car I owned at the time, an oath I soon forsook. While working at Columbia Records as a publicist, I told an associate about my teenage life of crime and how I was caught stealing that Five Shillings record and my desire to find it again. I discovered that it was now a very rare record and worth at least $40. I went into full panic mode as I realized that the music I'd grown up with might never be available to me again. I decided then and there to rebuild the collection regardless of the cost – and it did end up costing every spare moment.

During this time, I went from record company to record company taking jobs for free records, and finding free love as an additional bonus. For years, I had lived solely for the mania of the music; now the rest of the world was adopting the same lifestyle. The music and the musicians were accessible to everyone as the royal 'we' became the 'We' generation. The artists and the audiences seemed to have as much control of the music as the record industry did. There were even tribal gatherings called festivals that further united this musical movement. Pop music was so prevalent a part of pop culture that even *the* paramount pop artist, Andy Warhol, started designing album covers.

So, in 1977, I started the Michael Ochs Archives, a company devoted to preserving the musical past I loved so much. I continued getting every record released, and I started

collecting photographs, sheet music, concert program books – everything that could ef-
fectively document the continuing story of rock and roll. The friendship that had started in
my teenage years now blossomed into a marriage in the traditional sense of the word – till
death do us part.

The compilation of the many faces of rock and roll presented in this book is designed
to be as enjoyable as the music itself. This is neither a studious anthology of album cover
art nor a complete history, but rather a sampling of the album covers in my collection that
I felt would give a comprehensive picture of rock and roll from its infancy to the present.
The only criterion I used in this selection process was what caught my eye as being unique
and memorable for its time.

After pulling hundreds of album covers for the book, I tried to arrange them in some
order other than chronological. Besides the coupling of musical genres, I started to see
obvious patterns, such as the different depictions of blacks and women over the decades.
I realized that there are serious omissions in my selection, but that is the only serious limi-
tation of the book. Clearance problems and the peculiarities of my own taste inevitably
mean that a number of album covers that should be present here have not been included.
The method in my madness should be obvious from the layout of the covers – and my
apologies to all the great artists who did not survive the final cut.

I hope you enjoy this representative sampling of my favorite album covers as much as
I've enjoyed collecting them.

Michael Ochs
Venice, CA
December, 2000

Präludium

Als der Rock 'n' Roll und ich noch sehr jung waren, schlossen wir eine Freundschaft, die trotz vieler Höhen und Tiefen bis heute gehalten hat. Gleich nachdem ich ihn in den frühen 50er Jahren kennen gelernt hatte, war ich wild entschlossen, alles über meinen neuen Gefährten zu erfahren. Ich machte es mir zum Lebensziel, jede Platte zu hören, die je aufgenommen worden war. Heute beläuft sich meine Sammlung auf weit über 100.000 Platten und es wird zunehmend schwieriger, vor lauter Wald noch die Bäume zu sehen. Als ich einwilligte, das vorliegende Buch über Cover-Kunst zu machen, freute ich mich nicht nur darauf, die Bäume wieder zu sehen, sondern auch, auf die Wurzeln meiner Schallplattenmanie zurückzuschauen.

Die ersten Schallplatten, die ich in meinem Elternhaus Anfang der 50er Jahre kennen lernte, waren die Alben meines Vaters von Louis Armstrong, Louis Prima, Julie London und Doris Day. Ich hatte gerade erst das Teenageralter erreicht und kannte mich mit Prima und Armstrong noch nicht so gut aus, aber die Platten von Day und London fielen mir ins Auge und gingen mir ins Ohr. Nicht der Rock 'n' Roll war also meine erste Begegnung mit Erotik, sondern die Fotos der Dekolletés von Doris Day und Julie London auf ihren Schallplatten-covern.

Mein erstes Geld für Platten gab ich für Rock-'n'-Roll-Singles aus, die damals nur 89 Cent kosteten, Alben dagegen 3,98 Dollar. Mit 50 Cent Taschengeld die Woche war der Kauf von Schallplatten nicht einfach und so nahm meine kriminelle Karriere ihren Anfang. Ich baute einen kleinen Kasten mit doppeltem Boden, den ich mit in die Hörkabine im Platten-laden nahm. Auf jede Schallplatte, die ich vor den Augen der Verkäufer mit in die Kabine nahm, kamen drei bis vier, die wie von Zauberhand in dem Kasten verschwanden.

Ich hatte wohl schon Hunderte von Platten gestohlen, als meine Gier einfach zu groß wurde. Eines Tages hörte ich im Radio ein neues Stück mit dem Titel *Letter To An Angel* von den Five Shillings, und mir war sofort klar, dass ich die Platte so bald wie möglich im Laden stehlen musste. Es handelte sich um echte schwarze Musik und deshalb war nicht damit zu rechnen, dass sie lange im Radio gespielt oder auf dem Markt angeboten werden würde. Als ich den Laden betrat, war er leer. Mein Verstand sagte mir, dass es zu gefährlich sei, aber mein Herz obsiegte. Natürlich wurde ich erwischt. Die Verkäufer ließen mich laufen, nicht ohne vorher meine Eltern unterrichtet zu haben. Nachdem mein Vater mich gehörig bestraft hatte, bekam er Mitleid und erzählte mir, dass er sich in seiner Jugend auch keine neuen Platten leisten konnte und sie gebraucht bei Jukebox-Firmen gekauft hatte.

In der Woche darauf fuhr ich in die Stadt und ging zu allen Jukebox-Firmen, die ich finden konnte. Und tatsächlich, sie verkauften Singles für 25 Cent das Stück. Aber noch immer konnte ich mir nicht mehr als zwei Platten pro Woche leisten. Dann erfuhr ich, dass in dem Krankenhaus, in dem mein Vater arbeitete, ein Diskjockey lag, der unheilbar krank war. Ich besuchte ihn und fragte, ob er Lust habe, für die anderen Patienten über die Lautsprecheranlage des Krankenhauses eine Musiksendung zu machen. Er war begeistert und erklärte sich bereit, falls ich ihm ausreichend Schallplatten besorgen könnte.

Ich ging erneut zu den Jukebox-Firmen und brachte sie dazu, Schallplatten für das Krankenhaus zu spenden. Ich durfte sie zwar nicht behalten, aber schon bald hatte ich Woche für Woche vorübergehend einige Hundert Platten zu Hause. Als Teenager war es mir egal, ob ich die Platten besaß. Ich wollte so viel Musik wie möglich hören. Jetzt wusste ich, wie ich Singles umsonst bekam und noch dazu legal.

Die erste LP, die ich mir kaufte, war das zweite Album von Elvis Presley, nicht etwa, weil mir die erste Elvis-LP nicht gefiel, sondern weil ich die zweite in einem Haushaltswarengeschäft zum Angebotspreis von 1,98 Dollar statt der üblichen 3,98 Dollar entdeckte. Als ich mein erstes Album erstand, hatte ich in etwa das gleiche Gefühl wie beim ersten richtigen Kuss. Ich starrte auf das Cover-Foto eines strahlend lächelnden Elvis, klappte das Album auf und las die Titel auf der Hülle, streichelte das Cover, spähte in die Hülle, blickte auf die Platte, hielt inne und studierte dann wieder jeden Quadratzentimeter des Covers. Diese Vorfreude, bevor ich nach Hause kam und die Platte spielen konnte, war wunderbar. Zu meiner großen Überraschung war die ganze Platte eine Wucht, ohne einen einzigen Flop. Auf den meisten Rockalben, die ich bei Freunden gehört hatte, waren ein bis zwei Hits und ansonsten keine besonderen Songs. Schon bald sammelte ich Alben ebenso wie Singles.

Aus mehreren Gründen kamen mir LPs „erwachsener" vor als Singles. Alben wurden im Regal ausgestellt und verschwanden nicht in Sammelkartons. Sie waren nicht nur ein Hörerlebnis, sondern auch etwas fürs Auge; sie waren etwa 13 Zentimeter größer und viermal so teuer wie Singles. Man konnte das Plattencover in der Hand halten, während man die Musik hörte und man musste erst nach 20 Minuten die Platte umdrehen oder eine neue auflegen. Zu LPs hatte man eine Beziehung, mit Singles eine Affäre.

Die frühen Plattencover thematisierten das Amerika der unschuldigen Teenagerzeit. Der Rock 'n' Roll galt damals den Erwachsenen als viel zu stark sexuell aufgeladen, daher mussten die Cover absolut unverfänglich sein. Obwohl die frühen Musiker überwiegend schwarz waren, war das Amerika der Teenager eine weiße Welt. Die meisten Plattencover zeigten weiße Teenager in typischen Teenagerszenen. Erstaunlich ist, wie viele schwarze Künstler auf ihren Covern Fotos von Weißen hatten, während Fotos von Schwarzen, falls überhaupt vorhanden, auf die Rückseite verbannt wurden.

Obwohl der Rock 'n' Roll von schwarzen Musikern stammte, die dem Blues seinen Rhythmus verliehen hatten, versuchten Weiße, die Musik für sich zu vereinnahmen. Hinter vielen Songs von „unverfänglichen" weißen Künstlern wie Georgia Gibbs, Bill Haley, den McGuire Sisters und Pat Boone versteckten sich Originale von Schwarzen. Boone stahl seine Hits *Ain't That A Shame*, *At My Front Door*, *I'll Be Home* und *I Almost Lost My Mind* von schwarzen Sängern. Boone und Little Richard landeten beide mit Richards Song *Long Tall Sally* in den Hitparaden-Charts. Little Richard behauptete, dass Boone den Song unmöglich gestohlen haben konnte, da er, Richard, so schnell gesungen habe, dass Boone den Text gar nicht richtig mitkriegen konnte. Beim Vergleich des Fotos auf dem Cover des Little-Richard-Albums, auf dem sein schreiendes, schwitzendes Gesicht zu sehen ist, mit dem aseptischen Cover von Boone (ganz der adrette Collegejunge) sah die Käuferschicht der Teenager endlich ihre Wahlmöglichkeiten in lebendigem Schwarzweiß und Schwarz wurde bald die bevorzugte Farbe.

Doch gerade, als der Rock 'n' Roll so richtig in Schwung kam, schlug das Unglück zu. Little Richard fühlte sich von Gott berufen und kehrte der Teufelsmusik den Rücken zu, der populärste Rocker, Elvis Presley, wurde zur Armee eingezogen und Buddy Holly und Eddie Cochran kamen bei einem Flugzeugabsturz bzw. Autounfall ums Leben.

Obendrein kostete eine Schmiergeldaffäre Alan Freed die Karriere, einen der wildesten Diskjockeys im Land, der die größten und besten Rockkonzerte organisiert und sich sogar geweigert hatte, die weißen Cover-Versionen von schwarzen Hits zu spielen. Somit verkümmerte der Rock 'n' Roll Ende der 50er und Anfang der 60er Jahre zu harmlosen, maßgeschneiderten Teenageridolen wie Frankie Avalon, Fabian, Bobby Vee, Johnny Tillotson, Ricky Nelson und Bobby Rydell. Abgesehen von ihren „sauberen" Fotos auf den Covern, bescheinigte der Umschlagtext außerdem, dass diese Stars nicht bloß Rockmusiker waren – nein, sie waren auch bestrebt, über den Rock 'n' Roll hinauszuwachsen und studierten Schauspiel und Tanz.

Als der Rock 'n' Roll in den USA viel zu jung starb, ging die Saat auf, die Bill Haley, Eddie Cochran und Gene Vincent in England gestreut hatten, mit britischen Bands wie The Beatles, The Rolling Stones, The Animals, The Yardbirds und The Who. Und dann, als die 60er Jahre so richtig loslegten, verzweigten sich die Wurzeln des Rock 'n' Roll in alle Richtungen: Folk Rock, Surf, Soul, Psychedelic, Garage, Motown und die britische Invasion, all diese Elemente führten zusammen zu einer Rock-Revolution. Die Musik der amerikanischen Teenager war nun der Sound einer ganzen Generation und diese Generation war erwachsener und globaler. Die Plattencover spiegelten nun den Zeitgeist wider. Das Cover von Steve Millers erstem Album ließ sich nur entschlüsseln, wenn man bekifft war. David Bowie ließ sich für das Cover seines ersten Albums in einem Kleid ablichten und Jimi Hendrix wurde auf dem Cover (zumindest in England) von nackten Frauen umschwärmt.

Als ich das College verließ, hatte ich alle meine Platten verschenkt, bis auf etwa hundert meiner Lieblingsplatten. Wie ein richtiger Hippie der 60er Jahre schwor ich, niemals mehr besitzen zu wollen, als in den Kofferraum meines damaligen Wagens passte, ein Schwur, von dem ich mich bald wieder distanzierte. Bei Columbia erzählte ich einem Kollegen von meinen Diebstählen als Teenager, dass ich erwischt worden war, als ich eine Platte von den

Five Shillings klauen wollte, und dass ich diese Platte heute gerne wieder besitzen würde. Ich fand heraus, dass sie heute ein seltenes Sammlerstück war, und dass man 40 Dollar dafür zahlte – wenn man sie überhaupt auftreiben konnte. Ich bekam richtig Panik, als mir klar wurde, dass ich an die Musik, mit der ich groß geworden war, vielleicht nie wieder herankommen würde. Ich beschloss auf der Stelle, meine Sammlung wieder aufzubauen, koste es, was es wolle. Am Ende kostete es mich jede freie Minute.

Damals jobbte ich in verschiedenen Plattenfirmen, um Gratis-Schallplatten zu bekommen; als Dreingabe entdeckte ich die freie Liebe. Über Jahre habe ich nur für meine Musikbesessenheit gelebt. Die Musik und die Musiker waren jedem zugänglich, während aus dem „Wir" des Pluralis majestatis die demokratische Wir-Generation wurde. Die Künstler und ihr Publikum schienen die Musik ebenso sehr zu bestimmen wie die Plattenindustrie. Es fanden sogar Stammesfeste statt, genannt Festivals, auf denen die Musikbewegung noch stärker zusammengeschweißt wurde. Die Popmusik war ein so wesentlicher Teil der Popkultur, dass sogar der tonangebende Popkünstler Andy Warhol Plattencover gestaltete.

1977 eröffnete ich die Michael Ochs Archives, eine Firma, die sich der Bewahrung der von mir über alles geliebten Musikvergangenheit verschrieben hat. Ich verschaffte mir weiterhin jede Platte, die auf den Markt kam, und sammelte darüber hinaus Fotos, Noten, Konzertprogramme – einfach alles, was die Geschichte des Rock 'n' Roll anschaulich dokumentierte. Aus der Freundschaft, die in meiner Jugend begonnen hatte, war inzwischen eine Ehe geworden, im herkömmlichen Sinne des Wortes – bis dass der Tod uns scheidet.

Diese Zusammenstellung der vielen Gesichter des Rock 'n' Roll soll so unterhaltsam sein wie die Musik selbst. Sie will weder eine wissenschaftliche Anthologie der Kunst des Cover-Designs noch ein vollständiger Überblick über dessen Geschichte sein. Ich präsentiere Ihnen hier nur eine Auswahl der Cover aus meiner Sammlung, die meiner Ansicht nach einen Überblick über die Geschichte des Rocks von seinen Anfängen bis zur Gegenwart vermittelt. Meine Auswahl basiert auf dem, was mir persönlich als einzigartig und stellvertretend für seine Zeit ins Auge stach.

Nachdem ich Hunderte von LPs hervorgeholt hatte, versuchte ich, sie in eine Reihenfolge zu bringen, die über die bloße Chronologie hinausging. Neben der Zusammenstellung nach Musikrichtungen begann ich, offensichtliche Kriterien zu erkennen wie etwa die Veränderungen in den Darstellungen von schwarzen Musikern oder Frauen über Jahrzehnte hinweg. Ich stellte fest, dass in meiner Auswahl wichtige Platten fehlten, aber das ist der einzig ernsthafte Teil dieses Buches. Aufgrund meines abwegigen Musikgeschmacks wird sicherlich das eine oder andere Plattencover hier nicht abgebildet sein, das es verdient hätte. Die Methodik meiner Verrücktheit schlägt sich nieder im Layout der Cover und meine Entschuldigungen gelten all den großen Künstlern, die die endgültige Auswahl nicht überlebt haben.

Ich hoffe, Sie werden an dieser repräsentativen Auswahl aus meinen Lieblingscovern ebenso viel Freude haben wie ich, als ich sie sammelte.

Michael Ochs
Venice , Kalifornien
Dezember 2000

Lorsque nous étions très jeunes, le rock'n'roll et moi nous avons noué une amitié qui, malgré ses hauts et bas, a duré de longues années. Quand j'ai découvert le rock, au début des années cinquante, j'ai décidé que je voulais tout savoir de ce nouveau compagnon. Mon but dans la vie était d'écouter chaque disque de rock qui avait été produit. A présent que ma collection comprend bien plus de 100 000 disques, j'étais impatient de retrouver chacun d'eux et de remonter jusqu'aux racines de ma passion de collectionneur. Lorsque j'ai accepté de faire ce livre sur l'art des pochettes de disque, j'ai regardé en avant mais j'ai aussi regardé en arrière vers les racines de ma folie de collectionneur de disques.

Les premiers disques que je me rappelle avoir vus à la maison au début des années cinquante étaient des albums appartenant à mon père : Louis Armstrong, Louis Prima, Julie London et Doris Day. Au début de mon adolescence, je n'étais pas suffisamment dans le coup pour apprécier Prima et Armstrong, mais les disques de Doris Day et de Julie London, à défaut de séduire mon oreille, avaient franchement captivé mon regard. A vrai dire, je n'ai pas découvert la sexualité avec le rock'n'roll mais avec les pochettes très décolletées des albums de Day et de London.

Mes achats de disques ont commencé avec les 45 tours de rock'n'roll qui ne coûtaient que 89 cents, contrairement aux albums vendus $3,98. Avec 50 cents d'argent de poche par semaine, acheter des disques n'était pas facile, si bien que j'ai rapidement versé dans la délinquance. J'ai confectionné une petite boîte à double-fond que j'emportais dans la cabine d'écoute de mon disquaire de quartier. Pour chaque disque qu'il me voyait emporter dans la cabine, trois ou quatre autres disparaissaient magiquement dans la boîte.

J'ai bien dû voler des centaines de disques avant d'être victime de mon avidité. Un jour, j'ai entendu à la radio un nouveau disque intitulé *Letter To An Angel* par les Five Shillings et j'ai su que je devais le voler dès que possible : c'était un morceau de vraie musique noire qui allait être jugé trop « ethnique » et ne resterait pas longtemps sur les ondes. Il n'y avait pas d'autres clients lorsque je suis entré dans la boutique. Ma raison me soufflait que c'était trop dangereux, mais mon cœur a pris le dessus. Bien entendu, je me suis fait prendre. Le disquaire m'a finalement laissé partir, non sans avoir informé mes parents de mon crime. Après m'avoir puni, mon père compatissant m'a raconté que lorsqu'il était gosse et ne pouvait s'offrir de disques, il avait l'habitude d'en acheter d'occasion à des sociétés de juke-boxes.

Le week-end suivant, je me suis précipité en ville pour faire le tour de tous les loueurs de juke-boxes que j'avais pu trouver. Ils vendaient bien des 45 tours d'occasion à 25 cents pièce, mais je ne pouvais toujours pas m'en offrir plus de deux par semaine. J'ai alors appris que, dans l'hôpital où travaillait mon père, s'éteignait un disc-jockey atteint d'une maladie incurable. Je lui rendis visite et lui demandai s'il aimerait faire une émission de radio pour les autres malades en utilisant la sono de l'hôpital. Il me répondit qu'il adorerait le faire s'il y avait un moyen de se procurer des disques.

Je retournai voir tous les loueurs de juke-boxes et obtins d'eux qu'ils me donnent des disques pour l'hôpital. Bientôt des centaines de 45 tours transitèrent chaque semaine par ma maison. Adolescent, je voulais simplement écouter le plus de musique possible. Je savais désormais que je pouvais avoir des disques pour rien – en toute légalité.

Le premier 33 tours que j'ai acheté était le deuxième album d'Elvis Presley, non que je n'aie pas aimé le premier album, mais simplement parce que j'ai trouvé le deuxième soldé dans un bazar. En achetant mon premier album j'ai éprouvé un peu le même plaisir qu'en sortant pour la première fois avec une fille. Ah, l'anticipation sur le chemin du retour ! J'ai contemplé la magnifique photo d'Elvis sur la pochette, l'ai retournée pour lire les notes ; je l'ai caressée, j'ai glissé mon regard à l'intérieur pour regarder le vinyle, me suis arrêté et ai recommencé à en examiner chaque centimètre. Ce long préambule, avant même de rentrer pour poser le disque sur le plateau, était délicieux. A ma grande surprise, ce disque était passionnant d'un bout à l'autre, sans le moindre remplissage. Bientôt, je me mis à collectionner aussi des albums et pas seulement des 45 tours.

Pour toutes sortes de raisons, les albums paraissaient beaucoup plus « adultes » que les 45 tours. Ils étaient exposés sur des présentoirs et pas dans des bacs. De plus, ils ajoutaient à l'expérience auditive un plaisir visuel. Les albums étaient plus larges d'une douzaine de centimètres et quatre fois plus chers, on pouvait contempler la pochette en écoutant la musique, et chaque face durait presque vingt minutes. Aucune comparaison possible : dans un cas, il s'agissait d'une liaison éphémère et dans l'autre, d'une vraie relation amoureuse. Les premières pochettes étaient conçues pour captiver l'Amérique adolescente dans toute son innocence. Le rock était considéré comme trop sexualisé pour l'Amérique adulte, aussi les pochettes devaient-elles être pour la plupart cent pour cent anodines. Quoique la majorité des premiers musiciens de rock aient été noirs, l'Amérique adolescente était un monde blanc. C'est pourquoi la plupart des pochettes de disques montraient des adolescents blancs dans des scènes typiques de cet âge. On reste abasourdi en parcourant toutes ces pochettes de disques d'artistes noirs agrémentées de photos d'individus blancs au recto, alors que leurs propres portraits étaient, dans le meilleur des cas, relégués au verso.

Ce sont les noirs qui ont inventé le rock'n'roll en ajoutant le rythme au blues, mais les blancs se sont évertués à usurper cette musique. Beaucoup de morceaux de musique noire étaient repris par des artistes blancs comme Georgia Gibbs, Bill Haley, les McGuire Sisters et Pat Boone. Boone a fait des tubes avec des morceaux noirs tels que *Ain't That A Shame*, *At My Front Door*, *I'll Be Home* et *I Almost Lost My Mind*. Boone et Little Richard ont tous deux figuré en tête du Top 50 avec le *Long Tall Sally* du deuxième cité. En comparant la photo de pochette de Little Richard, le visage en sueur et hurlant, avec celle de Boone, entouré de camarades blancs, le public adolescent s'est vu proposer un choix en noir et blanc, et il a finalement préféré le noir.

Mais, juste au moment où le rock atteignait son apogée, le désastre est survenu : Little Richard a vu Dieu et il a renoncé à la musique du diable ; Elvis Presley a été appelé sous les drapeaux ; Buddy Holly et Eddie Cochran se sont tués respectivement en avion et en voiture.

Pour couronner le tout, un scandale de pots-de-vin a ruiné la carrière d'Alan Freed, l'un des disc-jockeys les plus sensationnels du pays. Il avait organisé les plus grands et les meilleurs concerts de rock et refusait même de passer les reprises blanches des succès noirs. Finalement, à la fin des années cinquante et au début des années soixante, le rock se réduisait au style anodin d'idoles d'adolescents fabriquées de toutes pièces comme Frankie Avalon, Fabian, Bobby Vee, Johnny Tillotson, Ricky Nelson, Bobby Rydell et consorts. Outre leurs photos innocentes sur les pochettes, les notes au verso insistaient sur le fait que ces artistes voulaient s'améliorer au-delà du rock en étudiant la comédie et la danse.

Tandis que le rock mourait prématurément aux Etats-Unis, les semences que Bill Haley, Eddie Cochran et Gene Vincent avaient plantées en Angleterre germaient avec des groupes comme les Beatles, les Rolling Stones, les Animals, les Yardbirds, les Who. Ensuite, quand les années soixante prirent réellement leur élan, le rock déploya des branches dans toutes les directions en même temps. Folk-Rock, Surf, Soul, Psychédélisme, Garage, Motown et Invasion Britannique s'unirent pour provoquer une révolution irrésistible. La musique des adolescents américains était devenue le son d'une génération plus mûre et plus universelle. Désormais, les pochettes de disques pouvaient vraiment refléter leur époque. Impossible de déchiffrer celle du premier album de Steve Miller, à moins d'être défoncé. David Bowie apparaissait en robe sur la pochette de son premier album, et Jimi Hendrix pouvait s'entourer d'un essaim de femmes nues sur la sienne – du moins en Angleterre.

En quittant l'université, j'ai bazardé tous mes disques, à l'exception d'une centaine de mes préférés. Dans le plus pur style hippie des années soixante, j'avais juré de ne rien posséder de plus que ce qui tiendrait dans la voiture que j'avais à cette époque. Un serment que j'ai très vite rompu. Après avoir raconté à l'un de mes collègues de Columbia ma vie d'adolescent délinquant, comment j'avais été pincé en volant ce disque des Five Shillings et combien j'aurais aimé le retrouver, j'ai découvert qu'il coûtait alors $40 ; à condition, bien entendu, d'avoir la chance de mettre la main dessus. J'ai été saisi de panique à l'idée que la musique avec laquelle j'avais grandi pourrait un jour devenir inabordable. J'ai décidé de rebâtir ma collection quoi qu'il en coûte, et j'ai fini par y consacrer tout mon temps libre.

A l'époque, je passais d'une maison de disques à l'autre, acceptant des boulots pour obtenir des disques gratuits et y trouvant l'amour libre en prime. Durant des années, la musique avait été mon unique passion, et je voyais le monde se rallier à mon mode de vie. Les musiciens et le public semblaient faire jeu égal avec l'industrie du disque dans le contrôle de la production musicale. Les rassemblements tribaux appelés festivals contribuaient à fédérer encore plus ce mouvement. La musique pop était si prédominante dans la culture pop que même Andy Warhol se mit à réaliser des pochettes d'albums.

En 1977, j'ai commencé à constituer les Archives Michael Ochs, une société dédiée à la conservation du passé musical que j'aime tant. J'ai continué à me procurer tous les nouveaux disques qui sortaient et j'ai commencé à collectionner photos, partitions, programmes de concerts – bref, tous les documents concernant l'histoire inachevée du rock.

Cette compilation des différents visages du rock'n'roll se veut aussi délectable que la musique elle-même. Il ne s'agit ni d'une anthologie méticuleuse de l'art des pochettes, ni d'une histoire exhaustive. Le lecteur y trouvera un échantillon des couvertures d'albums de ma collection offrant une vue d'ensemble du rock'n'roll. Seul critère de sélection : les pochettes qui m'avaient frappé comme uniques et mémorables pour leur époque.

J'ai essayé de déterminer un ordre autre que simplement chronologique. Outre le rapprochement par genres musicaux, j'ai commencé à voir certains fils conducteurs évidents tels les différentes représentations des noirs et des femmes à travers les décennies. Je me rends compte que ma méthode de sélection a entraîné de graves omissions, mais c'est bien le seul côté négatif de ce livre. En raison des difficultés de choix ou de la particularité de mes goûts, je suis sûr que de nombreuses pochettes qui sont absentes de ce livre auraient dû y figurer. La logique de ma folie devrait être évidente au vu des illustrations de pochettes. Toutes mes excuses à tous les grands artistes qui ont été éliminés au montage final.

J'espère que vous aimerez ce choix significatif de mes pochettes de disques préférées autant que j'ai aimé les collectionner.

Michael Ochs
Venice (Californie)
Décembre 2000

1950s

The 50s were the decade when all the war babies entered their teenage years. This new generation needed a new form of music to make their own. The big bands of the 40s were downsized into combos as solo singers and vocal groups became the new stars. While crooners and quartets dominated the charts, black 'race' records were becoming increasingly popular.

Rock and roll's birth certificate has never been found, so there is no definitive date for its birthday. Some say it all started in 1951 with Jackie Brenston's *Rocket 88* and The Dominoes' *Sixty Minute Man*, while others cite 1954 with The Chords' *Sh-Boom* and The Crows' *Gee*. To confuse the birth date further, Johnny Otis, Joe Turner, Roy Brown and Fats Domino all started recording before 1951. The early 50s were a magical music merging that created rock and roll by mixing gospel, blues, pop and country.

In the beginning the major record companies tried to ignore rock and roll, thinking it was a temporary aberration and would soon disappear. This gave rise to a number of independent record labels like Atlantic, Chess, Vee Jay and Specialty, that got their start by recording the early rockers. By the mid-50s rock and roll swept the nation as Bill Haley's *Rock Around The Clock* quickly became the biggest rock hit to date.

Rock and roll was often accused of being a plot to "lower" Whites to the level of the dreaded "Negro", but Elvis Presley proved that rock actually served to lift "The Man" culturally. Although Elvis started recording for Sun in 1954, he did not explode onto the national scene until he switched to RCA in 1956. In that year alone, Elvis had five number-one records, starred in the feature film *Love Me Tender* and appeared on national TV eleven times. The following year, rock and roll was seen regularly on TV as many local dance shows sprang up. Dick Clark's "American Bandstand" show was broadcast nationally every afternoon after school. Even the "Ozzie And Harriet" TV show began featuring Ricky Nelson songs weekly.

Toward the end of the 50s, rock and roll was losing its youthful exuberance. The pioneers of rock and roll were growing older and being replaced by safe and sanitized teenage idols.

Die 50er Jahre waren das Jahrzehnt, in dem die während des Krieges geborenen Kinder ins Teenageralter kamen. Die junge Generation verlangte nach einer neuen, eigenen Musikrichtung. Die Big Bands der 40er Jahre waren zu Combos verkümmert, während Solosänger und Gesangsgruppen zu den neuen Stars wurden. Während einerseits Schnulzensänger und Quartette die Hitlisten anführten, gewannen die so genannten Race Records der Schwarzen auf der anderen Seite zunehmend an Popularität.

Die Geburtsurkunde des Rock 'n' Roll ist bis heute verschollen, so dass sich nicht eindeutig bestimmen lässt, wann genau er seinen Anfang nahm. Einige meinen, dass alles im Jahr 1951 mit Jackie Brenstons *Rocket 88* und dem *Sixty Minute Man* von den Dominoes begann, andere hingegen verweisen auf *Sh-Boom* von den Chords und *Gee* von den Crows aus dem Jahr 1954. Für weitere Verwirrung sorgt die Tatsache, dass Johnny Otis, Joe Turner, Roy Brown und Fats Domino schon vor 1951 ihre ersten Schallplatten aufnahmen. Die frühen 50er Jahre wurden zu einem musikalischen Schmelztiegel, in dem sich so verschiedene Musikrichtungen wie Gospel, Blues, Pop und Country vermischten.

Zunächst schenkten die großen Plattenfirmen dem Rock 'n' Roll keine Beachtung, da sie ihn für eine kurzlebige Verirrung hielten. So entstanden etliche unabhängige Labels wie Atlantic, Chess, Vee Jay und Specialty Records, die sich mit Platten der frühen Rock-'n'-Roll-Künstler auf dem Markt etablierten. Doch schon Mitte der 50er Jahre löste der Rock 'n' Roll im ganzen Land Begeisterungsstürme aus, als Bill Haleys Platte *Rock Around The Clock* zum bis dahin erfolgreichsten Rock-Hit avancierte.

Man hat dem Rock 'n' Roll oft vorgeworfen, er würde die Weißen auf die Ebene der Schwarzen herabziehen, doch Elvis Presley bewies, dass der Rock 'n' Roll die Weißen vielmehr auf ebendiese Ebene emporhob. Obwohl Elvis schon 1954 seine erste Platte bei Sun herausgebracht hatte, wurde er erst 1956 mit seinem Wechsel zu RCA zum Superstar. Allein in diesem einen Jahr landete Elvis fünf Hits, spielte die Hauptrolle in dem Kinofilm „Love Me Tender" und trat elfmal im Fernsehen auf. Schon im Jahr darauf war Rock 'n' Roll aus dem Fernsehen nicht mehr wegzudenken. Viele regionale Tanzshows wurden ins Leben gerufen und Dick Clarks Show „American Bandstand" wurde jeden Nachmittag nach Schulschluss in die ganzen USA ausgestrahlt. Sogar die „Ozzie-and-Harriet"-Show hatte jede Woche Songs von Ricky Nelson im Programm.

Am Ende der 50er Jahre verlor der Rock jedoch sein jugendliches Feuer. Die Pioniere des Rock 'n' Roll wurden älter und durch etablierte, angepasste Teenageridole ersetzt.

Les années cinquante furent la décennie au cours de laquelle les enfants nés après la guerre entrèrent dans l'adolescence. Cette nouvelle génération avait besoin d'une nouvelle forme de musique qui lui appartienne. Les grands orchestres des années quarante se virent réduits à la portion congrue, tandis que les chanteurs et les groupes vocaux devenaient les nouvelles stars. Crooners et quatuors vocaux dominaient le Top 50 et les disques de « race » noire devenaient de plus en plus populaires.

On n'a jamais retrouvé l'acte de naissance du rock'n'roll, c'est pourquoi il est difficile de dater ses débuts avec exactitude. Certains disent que tout a commencé en 1951 avec *Rocket 88* de Jackie Brenston et *Sixty Minute Man* des Dominoes, alors que d'autres parlent de 1954 à cause de *Sh-Boom* des Chords et *Gee* des Crows. Pour compliquer encore cette datation, Johnny Otis, Joe Turner, Roy Brown et Fats Domino ont tous commencé à enregistrer avant 1951. Au début des années cinquante se produisit une fusion musicale magique qui créa le rock'n'roll en mélangeant gospel, blues, pop et country.

Les plus grandes maisons de disques ont d'abord essayé d'ignorer le rock'n'roll, convaincues qu'il s'agissait d'une complète aberration vouée à une disparition prochaine. Cette réticence a suscité l'apparition de nombreuses maisons de disques indépendantes comme Atlantic, Chess, Vee Jay et Specialty, qui ont toutes commencé en enregistrant les premiers rockers. Mais au milieu des années cinquante, lorsque *Rock Around The Clock* de Bill Haley est devenu le plus grand tube de l'histoire du rock, ce dernier a submergé l'Amérique.

Le rock a souvent été dénoncé comme un complot visant à *abaisser* l'homme blanc au niveau du « nègre », mais Elvis Presley a prouvé que le rock nous avait en fait *élevés* jusqu'à ce niveau. Quoiqu'Elvis ait commencé à enregistrer pour Sun en 1954, il n'explosa véritablement à l'échelon national qu'en 1956, lorsqu'il passa chez RCA. Durant cette seule année, Elvis signait cinq disques n°1 des ventes, tournait *Love Me Tender* (« Le Cavalier du Crépuscule »), et était programmé onze fois sur les écrans de la télévision nationale. L'année suivante, le rock faisait des apparitions régulières à la télévision tandis que débutaient de nombreuses émissions de danse locales et que le Dick Clark's « American Bandstand » Show était diffusé dans tout le pays chaque après-midi, après les cours. Même le « Ozzie and Harriet » Show se mit à présenter chaque semaine des chansons de Ricky Nelson.

Vers la fin des années cinquante, la musique rock avait perdu son exubérance juvénile et les pionniers du rock'n'roll vieillissant étaient peu à peu remplacés par des idoles convenables et inoffensives pour adolescents.

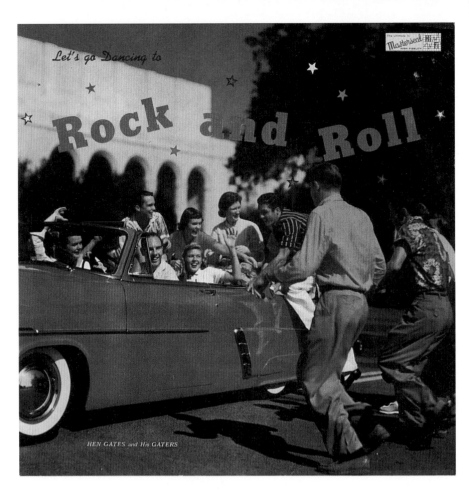

Hen Gates And His Gaters
Let's Go Dancing To Rock And Roll
Masterseal, 1957

Design: Unknown

Various Artists
Dance The Rock & Roll
Atlantic, 1957

Design: Unknown
Courtesy Atlantic Recording Corp.

The Robins
Rock & Roll With The Robins
Whippet, 1958

Design: Unknown

Frankie Laine
Rockin'
Columbia, 1957

Photo: John Engstead

Julie London
Julie Is Her Name
Liberty, 1956

Photo: Phil Howard

Johnnie Ray
Johnnie Ray
Columbia, 1951

Design: Unknown

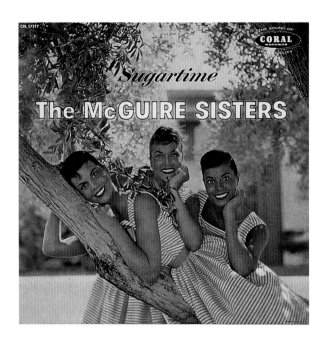

The McGuire Sisters
Sugartime
Coral, 1958

Photo: Garrett-Howard

The Four Coins
The Four Coins In Shangri-La
Epic, 1958

Design: Unknown

The Four Lads
The Four Lads Swing Along
Columbia, 1959

Design: Unknown

The Four Aces
The Swingin' Aces
Decca, 1958

Design: Unknown

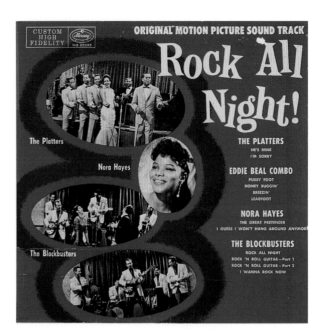

Various Artists
Rock All Night!
Mercury, 1958

Design: Unknown

Various Artists
Jamboree!
Warner Bros., 1955

Design: Unknown

The Crew Cuts
Rock And Roll Bash
Mercury, 1957

Design: Unknown

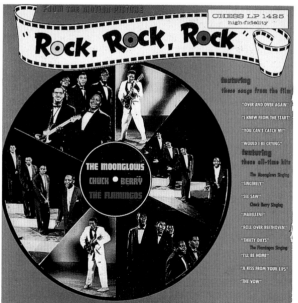

Various Artists
Rock, Rock, Rock
Chess, 1958

Design: Chuck Stewart

Various Artists
Rockin' Together
Atco, 1958

Design: Marvin Israel
Photo: Jules
Courtesy Atlantic Recording Corp.

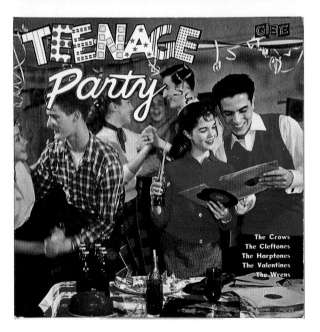

Various Artists
Teenage Party
Gee, 1958

Design: Lee-Miles Associates,
New York City

These compilations are of primarily black recording artists, yet, once again, only white people are shown on the covers.

Obwohl diese Alben überwiegend von schwarzen Musikern aufgenommen wurden, werden auf den Covern nur Weiße abgebildet.

Ces compilations contiennent essentiellement de la musique noire même si, une fois encore, seuls des blancs apparaissent sur les photos de pochettes.

Various Artists
Herald The Beat
Herald, 1960

Design: Unknown

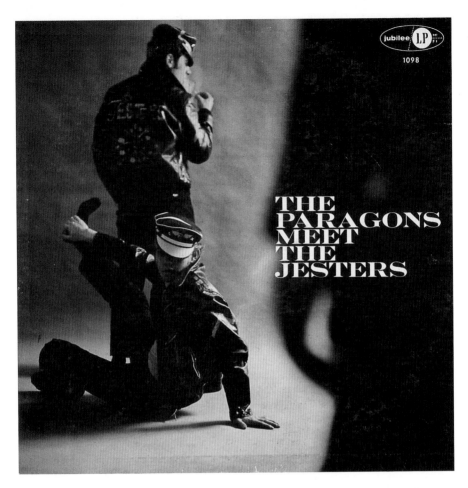

The Paragons/The Jesters
The Paragons Meet The Jesters
Jubilee, 1959

Design: Sy Leichman
Photo: Charles Varron

Not only do these compilations of black artists have white
people on the covers, but they also add to rock's dangerous
image by tying the music to juvenile delinquency.

Nicht nur, dass diese Alben schwarzer Künstler Weiße auf den
Covern zeigen, sie tragen außerdem zu dem schlechten Image
von Rockmusik bei, indem sie Jugendkriminalität damit in Ver-
bindung bringen.

Non seulement ces compilations de musique noire montrent
des blancs sur la pochette, mais elles contribuent à la mauvaise
image du rock en associant cette musique à la délinquance
juvénile.

Various Artists
Whoppers!
Jubilee, 1960

Design: Sy Leichman
Photo: Charles Varron

Various Artists
Boppin'!
Jubilee, 1961

Design: Sy Leichman/
Charles Varron

Lightnin' Hopkins
Lightnin' Hopkins
Folkways, 1962

Design: Ronald Clyne
Photo: Samul B. Charters

Reverend Gary Davis
Pure Religion!
Prestige, 1964

Design: Unknown

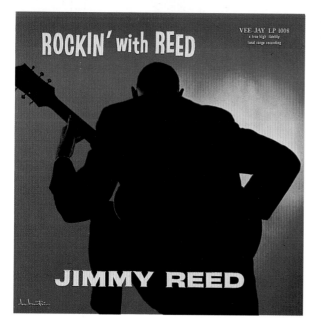

Jimmy Reed
Rockin' With Reed
Vee-Jay, 1959

Design: Don Bronstein

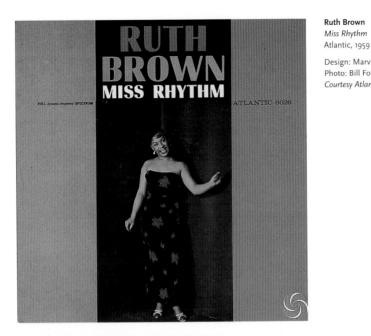

Ruth Brown
Miss Rhythm
Atlantic, 1959

Design: Marvin Israel
Photo: Bill Fotiades
Courtesy Atlantic Recording Corp.

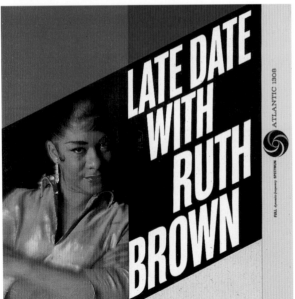

Ruth Brown
Late Date with Ruth Brown
Atlantic, 1959

Design: Marvin Israel
Photo: Bill Fotiades
Courtesy Atlantic Recording Corp.

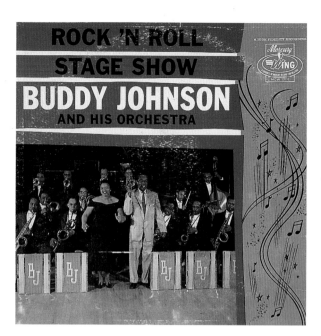

Buddy Johnson and His Orchestra
Rock 'N' Roll Stage Show
Mercury-Wing, 1956

Design: Unknown

LaVern Baker
La Vern
Atlantic, 1956

Design: Marvin Israel
Photo: Jerry Schatzberg
Courtesy Atlantic Recording Corp.

Cadets
Rockin' n' Reelin'
Crown, 1957

Art Direction: Florette Bihari
Photo: Gene Lesser, Hollywood

Two very rare picture covers soon replaced by covers with just drawings of the groups. Crown Records decided that photos were too costly for a budget label.

Diese beiden Cover sind eine Rarität. Crown Records fand, dass Fotos für ein Low-Budget-Label einfach zu teuer seien, und auf allen folgenden Alben fanden sich ausschließlich Zeichnungen von den Musikern.

Ces deux pochettes sont très rares car elles furent très vite remplacées par d'autres où ces groupes étaient représentés par des dessins. Crown Records estima que les photos étaient trop coûteuses et par la suite n'employa que ce type d'illustrations.

The Jacks
Jumpin' With The Jacks
Crown, 1956

Design: Unknown

The Chantels
We Are The Chantels
End, 1958

Design: Unknown

This original cover was changed soon after release and a white couple was put on the cover to get the record carried in the South. The original album is one of the rarest rock albums.

Das Foto der Mädchen auf dem Originalcover wurde rasch gegen die Abbildung eines weißen Pärchens ausgetauscht, um den Absatz im Süden der USA zu fördern. Das Originalalbum zählt zu den größten Raritäten der Rockmusik.

Le dessin des filles sur la pochette originale fut très vite remplacé après la sortie par un couple de blancs pour permettre au disque d'être distribué dans le Sud. La pochette originale avec les filles est l'un des albums de rock les plus rares.

The Chantels
The Chantels
End, 1950s

Design: Unknown

The Penguins
The Cool, Cool Penguins
Dooto, 1959

Design: Unknown

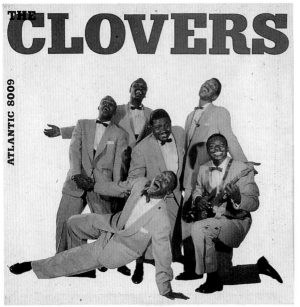

The Clovers
The Clovers
Atlantic, 1956

Design: Burt Goldblatt
Courtesy Atlantic Recording Corp.

The Spaniels
The Spaniels
Vee-Jay, 1950s

Design: Unknown

The Moonglows
Look! – It's The Moonglows
Chess, 1959

Design: Don Bronstein

The Platters
The Flying Platters Around The World
Mercury, 1959

Photo: Herman Leonard

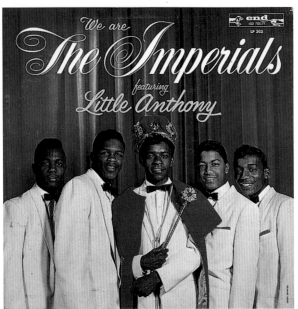

Little Anthony & The Imperials
We Are The Imperials Featuring Little Anthony
End, 1959

Design: Unknown

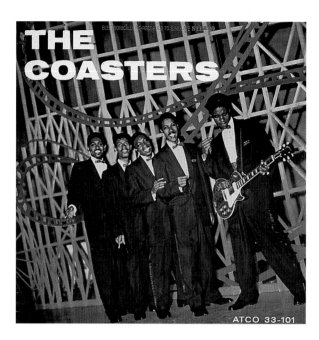

The Coasters
The Coasters
Atco, 1962

Design: Charles Varron
Courtesy Atlantic Recording Corp.

The Cadillacs
The Fabulous Cadillacs
Jubilee, 1957

Photo: Varron

Little Willie John
Fever
King, 1956

Design: Unknown

This is the super rare original cover with the white nurse. All other copies of this album just had the word "Fever" in big block type on the cover.

Hier handelt es sich um eine echte Rarität: das Originalcover mit der weißen Krankenschwester. Bei allen anderen Ausgaben dieses Albums steht bloß das Wort „Fever" in großen Blockbuchstaben auf dem Cover.

Ceci est la rarissime pochette originale avec l'infirmière blanche. Tous les autres exemplaires de ce disque portaient le mot « Fever » en très grosses lettres sur la pochette.

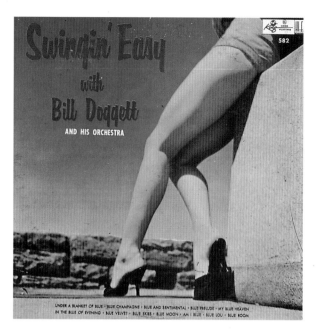

Bill Doggett And His Orchestra
Swingin' Easy
King, 1959

Design: Unknown

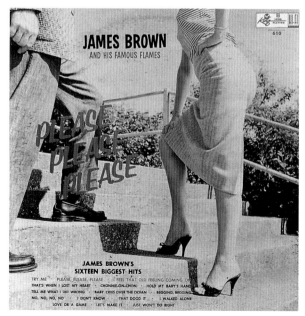

James Brown And His Famous Flames
Please, Please, Please
King, 1958

Design: Record Design Studio

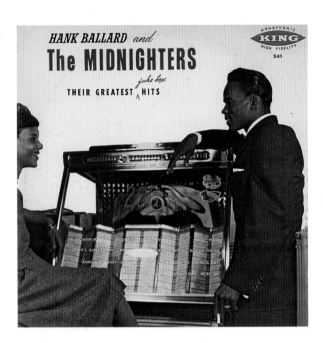

Hank Ballard And The Midnighters
Their Greatest Juke Box Hits
King, 1958

Design: Unknown

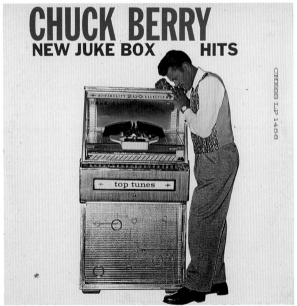

Chuck Berry
New Juke Box Hits
Chess, 1961

Design: Unknown

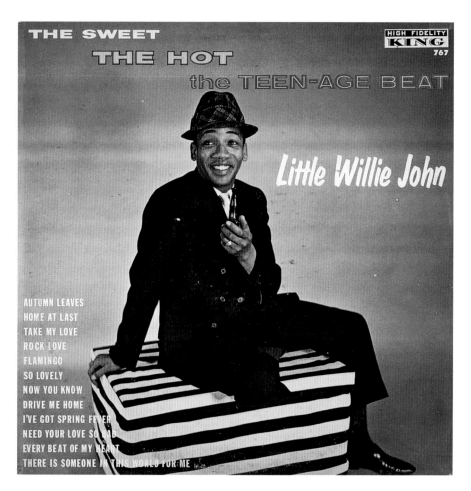

Little Willie John
The Sweet, The Hot, The Teen-Age Beat
King, 1961

Design: Unknown

Shep & The Limelites
Our Anniversary
Hull, 1962

Design: Unknown

Fats Domino
This Is Fats
Imperial, 1957

Design: Unknown

Fats Domino
Here Stands Fats Domino
Imperial, 1957

Design: Unknown

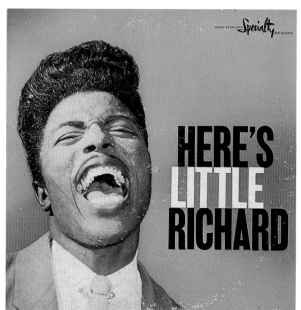

Little Richard
Here's Little Richard
Specialty Records, 1957

Design: Thadd Roark
Photo: Globe

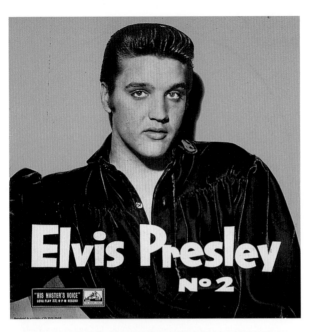

Elvis Presley
Elvis Presley N° 2
RCA/EMI International, 1956

Photo: Courtesy of The Daily Sketch
© Elvis Presley Enterprises, Inc.

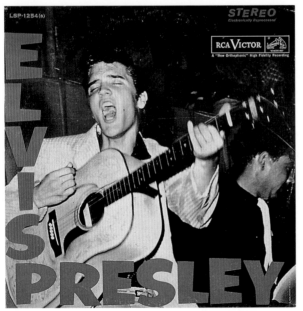

Elvis Presley
Elvis Presley
RCA Victor, 1956

Photo: Popsie
© Elvis Presley Enterprises, Inc.

Elvis Presley
50,000,000 Elvis Fans Can't Be Wrong
Elvis' Gold Records – Vol. 2
RCA Victor, 1960

Design: Unknown
© Elvis Presley Enterprises, Inc.

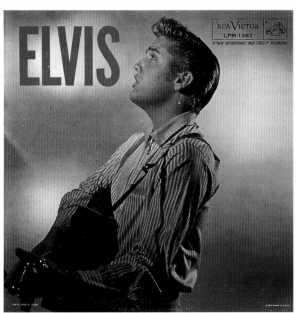

Elvis Presley
Elvis
RCA Victor, 1956

Design: Unknown
© Elvis Presley Enterprises, Inc.

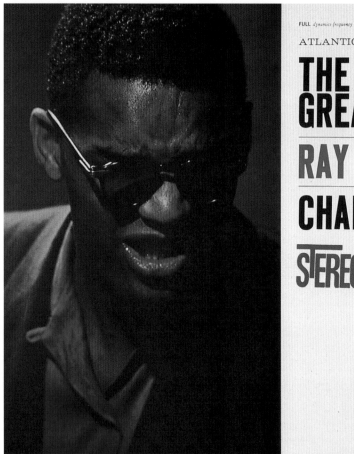

FULL *dynamics-frequency* SPECTRUM

ATLANTIC 1259

THE GREAT RAY CHARLES

STEREO

Ray Charles
The Great Ray Charles
Atlantic, 1959

Design: Marvin Israel
Photo: Lee Friedlander
Courtesy Atlantic Recording Corp.

This original cover was later changed to *Twist With Ray Charles* to capitalize on the Twist craze as was done with the surf and folk fads.

Das Originalcover bekam später den Titel *Twist With Ray Charles*, um von der Twist-Welle zu profitieren, wie man es zuvor schon bei der Surf- und Folk-Welle praktiziert hatte.

Cette pochette originale fut plus tard transformée en *Twist With Ray Charles* afin de tirer profit de la folie du twist, de la même façon qu'on l'avait fait avec les modes surf et folk.

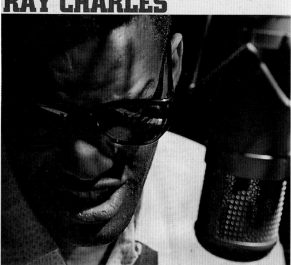

Ray Charles
What'd I Say
Atlantic, 1959

Design: Marvin Israel
Photo: Lee Friedlander
Courtesy Atlantic Recording Corp.

Ray Charles
Ray Charles At Newport
Atlantic, 1958

Design: Marvin Israel
Photo: Lee Friedlander
Courtesy Atlantic Recording Corp.

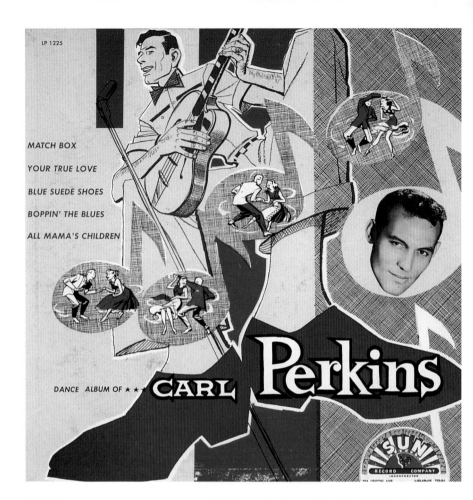

LP 1225

MATCH BOX

YOUR TRUE LOVE

BLUE SUEDE SHOES

BOPPIN' THE BLUES

ALL MAMA'S CHILDREN

DANCE ALBUM OF ★ ★ CARL Perkins

Carl Perkins
Dance Album Of Carl Perkins
Sun, 1957

Design: Unknown
Courtesy Sun Entertainment Corporation

This is the rare first cover of Carl's *Teen Beat* Sun Records album.

Das seltene erste Cover von Carls Sun-Records-Album *Teen Beat*.

Ceci est la très rare première pochette de l'album de Carl *Teen Beat* pour Sun Records.

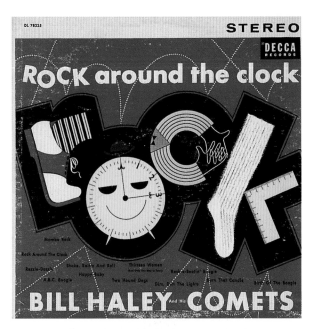

Bill Haley And His Comets
Rock Around The Clock
Decca, 1956

Design: Unknown

Jerry Lee Lewis
Jerry Lee Lewis
Sun, 1958

Design: Unknown
*Courtesy Sun Entertainment
Corporation*

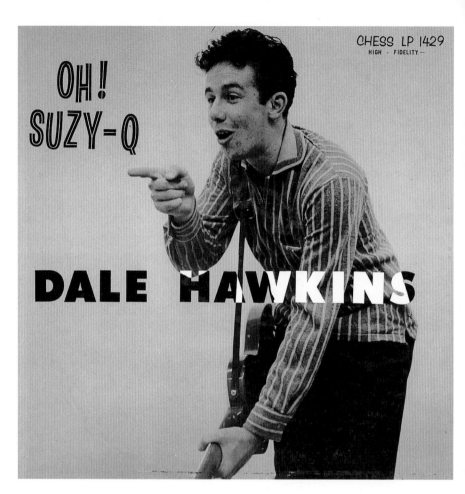

Dale Hawkins
Oh! Suzy-Q
Chess, 1958

Design: Unknown

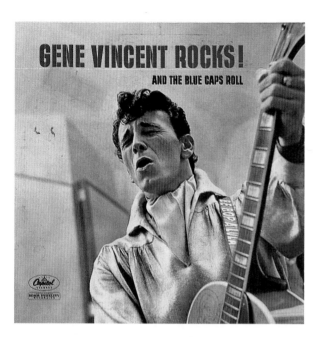

Gene Vincent And The Blue Caps
Gene Vincent Rocks! And The Blue Caps Roll
Capitol, 1958

Design: Unknown

Gene Vincent And The Blue Caps
Gene Vincent And The Blue Caps
Capitol, 1957

Design: Unknown

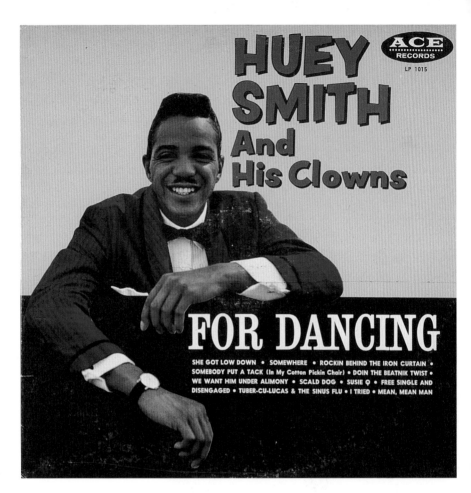

Huey Smith And His Clowns
For Dancing
Ace, 1961

Design: Unknown

Johnny Otis
The Johnny Otis Show
Capitol, 1958

Design: Unknown

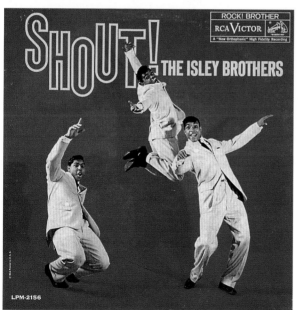

The Isley Brothers
Shout!
RCA Victor, 1959

Design: Unknown

Bobby Day
Rockin' With Robin
Chess, 1959

Design: Unknown

Dee Clark
Dee Clark
Abner, 1959

Photo: Don Bronstein

Jackie Wilson
He's So Fine
Brunswick, 1959

Design: Unknown

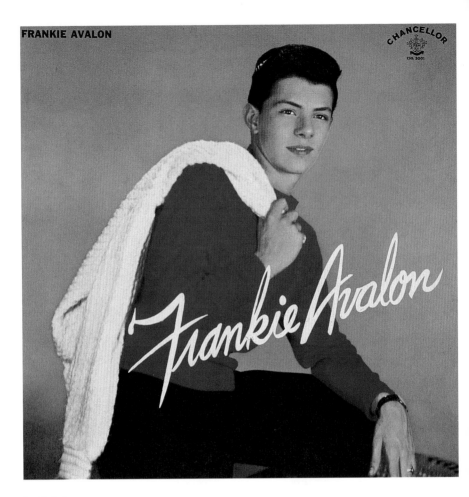

Frankie Avalon
Frankie Avalon
Chancellor, 1958

Photo: Bob Ghiraldini/Arsene Studios,
New York

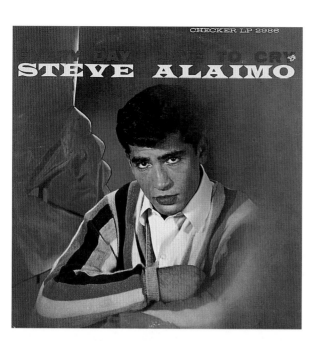

Steve Alaimo
Every Day I Have To Cry
Checker, 1963

Design: Howard Richmond

Fabian
Hold That Tiger!
Chancellor, 1959

Photo: Marvin Wellen/Topix

The Four Lovers
Joyride
RCA Victor, 1956

Design: Unknown

This is the first album Frankie Valli (on the far left) recorded before forming the Four Seasons.

Dies ist das erste Album, das Frankie Valli (links außen) aufgenommen hat, bevor er die Four Seasons gründete.

Ceci est le premier album qu'enregistra Frankie Valli (à gauche) avant de former les Four Seasons.

Phil Spector (on the far right) was the leader of The Teddy Bears.

Phil Spector (ganz rechts) war der Bandleader der Teddy Bears.

Phil Spector (à l'extrême droite) était le leader des Teddy Bears.

The Teddy Bears
The Teddy Bears Sing!
Imperial, 1959

Photo: Garrett-Howard

1960s

The 60s were the war years – and not just in Vietnam. In America, there was a full-tilt war between adolescence and age – it was US against THEM. US had long hair, free love, expanded consciousness, new highs, new lows, new clothes and new music. THEM was stunting, straight, selfish, archaic and imperialistic. All this was communicated through the expanding music scene.

As the teen idol and twist trends were strangling the life out of rock and roll, fresh sounds surfaced at home and abroad. In 1961, Bob Dylan played his first professional gig at Gerde's in New York and The Beatles opened at the Cavern in Liverpool. From the roots of American music a musical revolution sprang – a global battle of the bands in which growth and change won the day. Every branch of rock and roll soared to incredible heights.

In 1962, The Beach Boys rode the first wave of the revolution with their hit *Surfin' Safari*, which started the fun-in-the-sun sound. Berry Gordy launched his Motown Records with hits by the Miracles, Mary Wells and The Marvelettes. Black novelty records by groups like The Coasters and The Olympics were soon replaced by the more soulful sounds of the streets, with artists like Wilson Pickett, Gladys Knight, Otis Redding and Etta James.

In 1964, *Meet The Beatles* was released in America, and the whole country met The Beatles on the February 9th "Ed Sullivan" TV show. During that year, the British invasion dominated the American hit parade with the debut records of The Animals, The Dave Clark Five, Gerry and The Pacemakers, The Hollies, The Kinks, Manfred Mann, The Rolling Stones, The Searchers and The Zombies.

The psychedelic revolution started in San Francisco with The Grateful Dead and The Jefferson Airplane. Not to be outdone, Los Angeles added The Doors and Love. New York swelled the ranks with the Velvet Underground and Vanilla Fudge. The Brits countered with a leaner, meaner second wave of invasion bands like The Who and The Yardbirds.

As the decade came to a close, the war years were finally coming to an end. However, the casualty rate was staggering with Jimi Hendrix, Janis Joplin and Jim Morrison all dying at the age of 27.

Die 60er Jahre standen im Zeichen des Krieges und das nicht nur in Vietnam. In den USA kam es zu einem regelrechten Krieg zwischen den Generationen – auf der einen Seite standen die SPIESSER, auf der anderen Seite WIR. WIR, das bedeutete lange Haare, freie Liebe, Bewusstseinserweiterung, Hochs und Tiefs, neue Kleidung und neue Musik. Die SPIESSER waren verknöchert, kleinkariert, egozentrisch, altmodisch und imperialistisch. Das alles schlug sich in der immer vielfältigeren Musikszene nieder.

Während die Teenageridole und der Twist dem Rock 'n' Roll den Lebensnerv abschnürten, zeichneten sich in den USA und anderswo ganz neue Musikrichtungen ab. 1961 hatte Bob Dylan seinen ersten professionellen Gig im New Yorker Gerde's und die Beatles gaben im Cavern Club in Liverpool ihr Debüt. Die Musik, die in den USA wurzelte, führte nun zu einer echten musikalischen Revolution, einem weltweiten „Sängerstreit" der Rockgruppen, bei dem die musikalische Weiterentwicklung den eigentlichen Sieg davontrug. Jede Spielart des Rock 'n' Roll erreichte im Verlauf dieser Revolution ein bis dato ungeahntes Niveau.

1962 ritten die Beach Boys auf der ersten Welle der Revolution mit ihrem Hit *Surfin' Safari* und begründeten den „Fun-in-the-Sun"-Sound. Berry Gordy hob seine Plattenfirma Motown Records aus der Taufe und erreichte mit Hits von The Miracles, Mary Wells und The Marvelettes einen kometenhaften Aufstieg. An die Stelle neuer Platten von schwarzen Gruppen wie The Coasters und The Olympics trat schon bald der stark am Soul orientierte Sound der Straße von Sängern wie Wilson Pickett, Gladys Knight, Otis Redding und Etta James.

1964 kam in den USA das Album *Meet The Beatles* heraus und am 9. Februar des Jahres konnten alle US-Bürger die Beatles in der „Ed-Sullivan-Show" im Fernsehen kennen lernen. Im Lauf desselben Jahres kam es in der amerikanischen Hitparade zu einer regelrechten britischen Invasion, denn Gruppen wie The Animals, The Dave Clark Five, Gerry and The Pacemakers, The Hollies, The Kinks, Manfred Mann, The Rolling Stones, The Searchers und The Zombies landeten mit ihren Debütplatten auf den ersten Plätzen.

Die psychedelische Revolution begann in San Francisco mit The Grateful Dead und The Jefferson Airplane. Los Angeles ließ sich nicht lumpen und mobilisierte The Doors und Love. New York ließ Velvet Unterground und Vanilla Fudge aufmarschieren. Die Briten reagierten mit einer schwächeren, bissigen Gegenoffensive und schickten Gruppen wie The Who und The Yardbirds ins Feld.

Am Ende des Jahrzehnts wurde der Krieg endgültig beigelegt, doch mit erschütternden Verlusten: Jimi Hendrix, Janis Joplin und Jim Morrison waren alle drei im Alter von 27 Jahren gestorben.

Les années soixante furent les années de guerre – et pas seulement au Vietnam. En Amérique, la guerre sévissait entre jeunes et adultes – c'était NOUS contre EUX. NOUS avions opté pour les cheveux longs, l'amour libre, la « conscience élargie », de nouveaux hauts et bas, de nouveaux vêtements et une nouvelle musique. EUX étaient desséchés, sérieux, égoïstes, archaïques et impérialistes. Cette vision du monde s'exprimait dans la musique qui jouait un rôle de plus en plus important.

Alors que les idoles des adolescents et les adeptes du twist étaient en train d'étouffer le rock'n'roll, des sonorités nouvelles firent leur apparition chez nous et de l'autre côté de l'Atlantique. En 1961, Bob Dylan donnait son premier récital chez Gerde's à New York, et les Beatles faisaient l'ouverture de la Cavern à Liverpool. Sous l'influence de la musique américaine éclatait une révolution musicale, une guerre totale des groupes qui se solda par une accélération et un renouveau spectaculaire : toutes les expressions du rock'n'roll se propulsaient vers des sommets inédits.

En 1962, les Beach Boys surfèrent sur la première vague de la révolution avec leur tube *Surfin' Safari*, lançant le son « fun-in-the-sun ». Berry Gordy lançait sa marque Motown Records avec des tubes des Miracles ou de Mary Wells et ses Marvelettes. Les disques de nouveautés noires de groupes comme les Coasters et les Olympics furent bientôt remplacés par les sons de la rue beaucoup plus inspirés d'artistes comme Wilson Pickett, Gladys Knight, Otis Redding et Etta James.

En 1964, le disque *Meet The Beatles* sortit aux Etats-Unis, et tout le pays rencontra effectivement les Beatles dans le « Ed Sullivan » TV Show du 9 février. Cette année-là, l'Invasion Britannique domina le hit-parade américain avec les premiers disques des Animals, du Dave Clark Five, de Gerry and The Pacemakers, des Hollies, des Kinks, de Manfred Mann, des Rolling Stones, des Searchers et des Zombies.

La révolution psychédélique commençait à San Francisco avec le Grateful Dead et Jefferson Airplane. Pour ne pas être en reste, Los Angeles ajouta les Doors et Love. New York grossit les rangs avec le Velvet Underground et Vanilla Fudge. Les Anglais réagirent par une seconde vague moins imposante de groupes envahisseurs comme les Who et les Yardbirds.

Avec le début des années soixante-dix, les années de guerre touchaient à leur fin. Pourtant, la liste des victimes s'allongeait de façon vertigineuse avec les disparitions de Jimi Hendrix, Janis Joplin et Jim Morrison, tous les trois âgés de vingt-sept ans.

The Olympics
Doin' The Hully Gully
Arvee, 1960

Design: Unknown

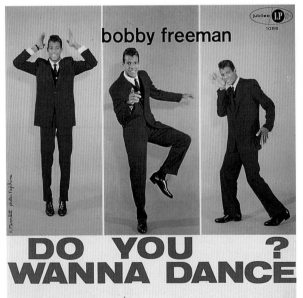

Bobby Freeman
Do You Wanna Dance?
Jubilee, 1959

Design: Harry Farmlett
Photo: Fujihira

Johnny Thunder
Loop De Loop
Diamond, 1963

Art Direction: Arnold Meyers

The Flares
Encore Of Foot Stompin' Hits
Press, 1961

Design: Unknown

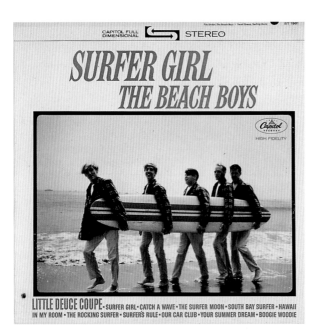

The Beach Boys
Surfer Girl
Capitol, 1963

Design: Capitol Photo Studio/
Ken Veeder

The Beach Boys
Surfin' Safari
Capitol, 1962

Photo: Capitol Photo Studio/
Ken Veeder

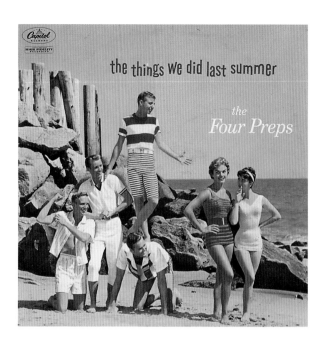

The Four Preps
The Things We Did Last Summer
Capitol, 1958

Design: Unknown

Jan & Dean
Jan & Dean Take Linda Surfin'
Liberty, 1963

Design: Studio Five

The Simon Sisters
Cuddlebug
Kapp, 1964

Photo: Alex Greco

Carly and her sister Lucy had a few hits as a duo before Carly's solo career took off.

Carly und ihre Schwester Lucy landeten als Duo ein paar Hits, bevor Carlys Solokarriere begann.

Carly et sa sœur Lucy eurent quelques hits en duo avant que la première ne démarre une carrière solo.

Judy Collins
Judy Collins #3
Elektra, 1964

Design: William S. Harvey
Photo: Jim Marshall
Courtesy Elektra Entertainment Group

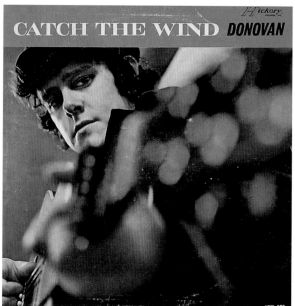

Donovan
Catch The Wind
Hickory, 1965

Design: Unknown

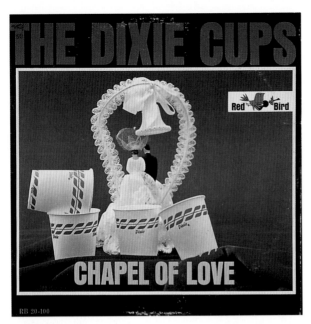

The Dixie Cups
Chapel Of Love
Red Bird, 1964

Design: Loring Eutemey
Photo: Hugh Bell

The Shirelles
Tonight's The Night
Scepter, 1961

Design: Lee-Miles Associates,
New York City

Bob B. Soxx And The Blue Jeans
Zip-A-Dee Doo Dah
Philles Records (Phil Spector Records, Inc.),
1963

Design: Bob Abrams
© Phil Spector Records, Inc.

The Shirelles
Foolish Little Girl
Scepter, 1963

Design: Unknown

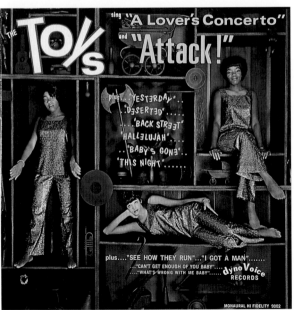

The Toys
*The Toys Sing "Lover's Concerto" And
"Attack!"*
Dynovoice, 1966

Design: Bob Crewe
Photo: Ron Harris

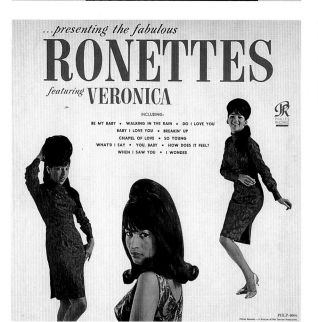

The Sherrys
At The Hop With The Sherrys
Guyden, 1962

Photo: Michael Denning

The Ronettes
… Presenting The Fabulous Ronettes Featuring Veronica
Philles Records (Phil Spector Records, Inc.), 1964

Design: Three Lions Studio
© Phil Spector Records, Inc.

James Brown
*James Brown Presents
His Show Of Tomorrow*
King, 1968

Design: Unknown

James Brown
*I Can't Stand Myself
When You Touch Me*
King, 1968

Design: Roger McElya

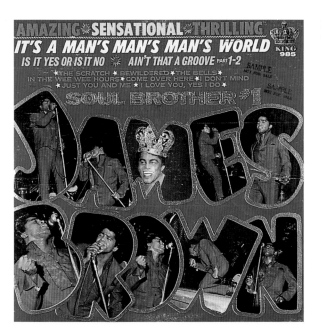

James Brown
It's A Man's Man's Man's World
King, 1966

Design: Unknown

James Brown
Showtime
Smash, 1964

Design: Unknown

Dee Clark
Hold On ... It's Dee Clark
Vee-Jay, 1961

Design: Unknown

Jerry Butler
Aware Of Love
Vee-Jay, 1961

Design: Unknown

All three of these black artists (Clark, Butler, Henry) had generic
white people on their album covers.

Alle drei schwarzen Künstler (Clark, Butler, Henry) hatten Weiße
auf den Covern ihrer Alben.

Ces trois artistes noirs (Clark, Butler, Henry) eurent des individus blancs sur leur pochette d'album.

Clarence Henry
You Always Hurt The One You Love
Argo, 1961

Design: Unknown

Mary Wells
The One Who Really Loves You
Motown, 1962

Design: Barni Wright

Berry Gordy's Motown Records put generic cartoons on these early record covers to appeal to a teenage America.

Berry Gordys Motown Records gestaltete diese frühen Plattencover mit Cartoons, um bei den amerikanischen Teenagern anzukommen.

La Motown Records de Berry Gordy mit des personnages de dessins animés sur les pochettes de ses premiers albums afin de séduire les adolescents américains.

The Marvelettes
Please Mr. Postman
Tamla, 1961

Design: Barni

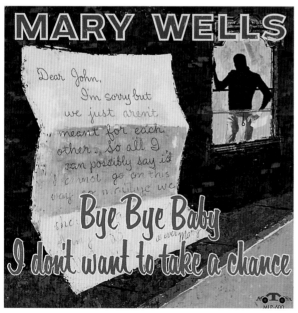

Mary Wells
Bye Bye Baby/
I Don't Want To Take A Chance
Motown, 1961

Design: Barni

Ike & Tina Turner
Ike & Tina Turner's Kings Of Rhythm Dance
Sue, 1962

Design: Unknown

Ike & Tina Turner
Dynamite!
Sue, 1963

Design: Unknown

Inez & Charlie Foxx
Inez & Charlie Foxx
Sue, 1966

Design: Frank Lerner
Photo: Richard Litwin

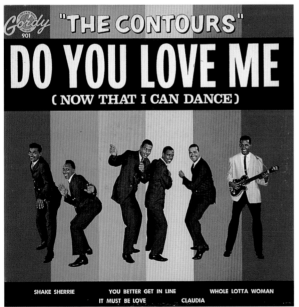

The Contours
Do You Love Me (Now That I Can Dance)
Gordy, 1962

Design: Barni Wright

DS-50006

•••••••••STEREO•••••••••

DUNHILL

THE MAMA'S AND THE PAPA'S

IF YOU CAN BELIEVE YOUR EYES AND EARS

The Mama's And The Papa's
If You Can Believe Your Eyes And Ears
Dunhill, 1966

Photo: Guy Webster

This is one of the only rock albums that had three covers. The original and the second cover were considered too dirty. So the third cover was created blocking out the whole bathroom motif.

Eines der wenigen Rockalben, das drei Cover hatte. Das Original und das zweite Cover wurden als zu unanständig empfunden. So schuf man das dritte Cover, auf dem das Badezimmermotiv verschwand.

Ceci est l'un des seuls albums de rock à avoir eu trois pochettes. La pochette originale et la seconde furent jugées trop dégoûtantes. Sur la troisième pochette, le motif de la salle de bains avait disparu.

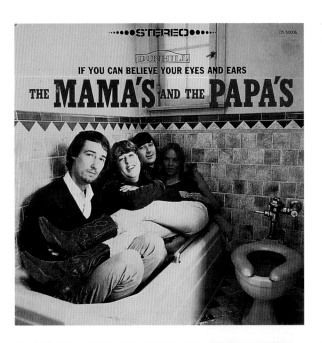

The Mama's And The Papa's
If You Can Believe Your Eyes And Ears
Dunhill, 1966

Photo: Guy Webster

The Mama's And The Papa's
If You Can Believe Your Eyes And Ears
Dunhill, 1966

Photo: Guy Webster

Dr. Timothy Leary PH.D.
L.S.D.
Pixie, 1966

Design: Unknown

As part of the acid rock movement, even Timothy Leary cranked out a couple of albums. This is the better cover of the two.

Als Teil der Acid-Rock-Bewegung brachte sogar Timothy Leary zwei Alben heraus. Dies ist das bessere der beiden Cover.

Figure clé du mouvement acid rock, Timothy Leary sortit lui-même deux albums. Cette pochette est la meilleure des deux.

The Thirteenth Floor Elevators
The Psychedelic Sounds Of 13th Floor Elevators
International Artists, 1967

Design: John Cleveland, Austin (Texas)
International Artists Courtesy Of Charly Records

Vanilla Fudge
Vanilla Fudge
Atco, 1967

Design: Haig Adishian
Photo: Bruce Laurance
Courtesy Atlantic Recording Corp.

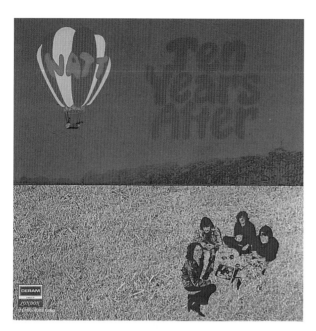

Ten Years After
Watt
Deram, 1960s/70s

Design: John Fowlie
Color Processing: Graham Nash

The Steve Miller Band
Children Of The Future
Capitol, 1968

Design: Victor Moscoso
Photo: Elaine Mayes

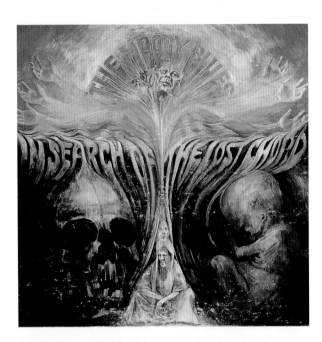

The Moody Blues
In Search Of The Lost Chord
Deram, 1968

Design: Philip Travers

Neil Young
Neil Young
Reprise, 1968

Art Direction: Neil Young
Portrait: Roland Diehl

Moby Grape
Wow
Columbia, 1968

Design: Bob Cato

Mike Bloomfield & Al Kooper
The Live Adventures Of Mike Bloomfield & Al Kooper
Columbia, 1969

Design: Virginia Team
Painting: Norman Rockwell

Joni Mitchell
Clouds
Reprise, 1969

Art Direction: Ed Thrasher
Painting: Joni Mitchell

Bob Dylan
Self Portrait
Columbia, 1970

Design: Ron Coro
Painting: Bob Dylan

Freddie Hughes
Send My Baby Back
Scepter, 1968

Design: Burt Goldblatt

Eddie Floyd
Knock On Wood
Stax, 1967

Design: Ronnie Stoots

Otis Redding
The Otis Redding Dictionary Of Soul
Volt, 1966

Design: Ronnie Stoots

Sam & Dave
Hold On, I'm Comin'
Stax, 1966

Design: Ronnie Stoots

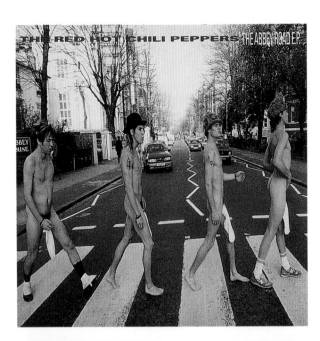

Red Hot Chili Peppers
The Abbey Road EP
EMI-Manhattan, 1988

Design: Abrahams Pants
Photo: Chris Clunn

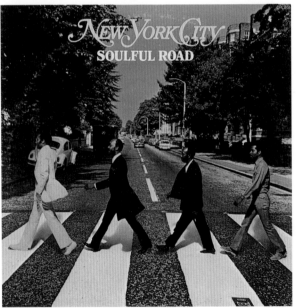

New York City
Soulful Road
Chelsea, 1973

Design: Big Cigar
Photo: Ian MacMillian

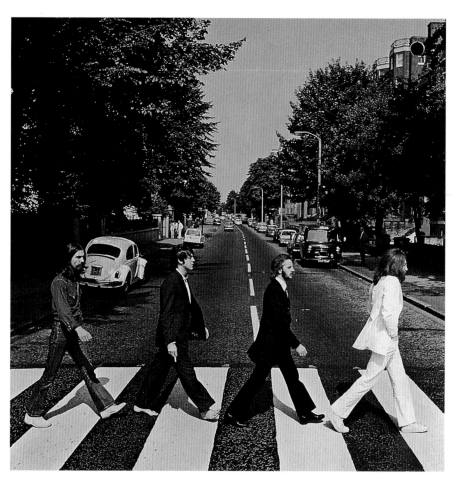

The Beatles
Abbey Road
Capitol/EMI, 1969

Photo: Iain MacMillan
© Apple Corps Ltd.

Blind Faith
Blind Faith
Atco, 1969

Design: Bob Seidemann
Courtesy Atlantic Recording Corp.

Although this cover was banned and replaced by another cover, this is still the most common copy of the album.

Obwohl das Plattencover verboten und durch ein anderes ersetzt wurde, ist es immer noch die am meisten verbreitete Version des Albums.

Bien que cette pochette ait été interdite et remplacée par une autre, il s'agit pourtant de la version la plus répandue de cet album.

The Grape was one of the most highly touted San Francisco bands that failed to sell. This album was banned before the offending finger over the washboard was air-brushed out.

The Grape war eine der Bands aus San Francisco, für die sehr viel Werbung gemacht wurde, ohne dass es sich finanziell auszahlte. Dieses Album war verboten, bis der anstößige Finger über dem Waschbrett wegretuschiert wurde.

The Grape, l'un des groupes les plus branchés de San Francisco, ne connut jamais de succès commercial. Cet album fut interdit jusqu'à ce que le doigt offensant sur la planche à laver eût été supprimé.

Moby Grape
Moby Grape
Columbia, 1967

Photo: Jim Marshall

The Jimi Hendrix Experience
Electric Ladyland
Track, 1968

Design: David King
Photo: David Montgomery

THE JIMI HENDRIX EXPERIENCE ELECTRIC LADYLAND

This cover with the nude women was banned in the USA and
only released in Europe.

Dieses Cover mit den nackten Frauen war in den USA verboten
und erschien nur in Europa.

La prochette avec les femmes nues fut interdite aux Etats-Unis
et ne sortit qu'en Europe.

1970s

After the unconditional surrender of the US-generation of the 60s, the ME-generation of
the 70s came to power. As the war babies entered their thirties, WE started to become
THEM. The sound of a generation was splintered into various musical genres that reflected
narcissism rather than idealism.

The first trend of the 70s seemed to be the dismantling of successful 60s bands. In
1970, The Beatles broke up to pursue separate careers. In 1971, Michael Jackson and Rod
Stewart scored their first hits without their groups and joined the swelling ranks of solo
singing stars such as Elton John, Billy Joel, Cat Stevens, James Taylor and Jim Croce. In
addition, many female singers such as Linda Ronstadt, Carly Simon, Carole King and Olivia
Newton-John became stars in their own right. For those wanting more diverse forms of
music, Led Zeppelin and Kiss kept the heavy-metal sound alive, while Marc Bolan, David
Bowie and The New York Dolls invented glitter rock. The progressive rock bandwagon was
represented by Yes, Roxy Music and Pink Floyd.

The splintering rock scene of the 70s was united commercially with the release of the
disco-dance film *Saturday Night Fever*. The accompanying album could not be manufactured fast enough to meet the demand and, with 25 million copies sold, soon became the
biggest selling soundtrack album of all time. Gloria Gaynor, The Village People and Donna
Summer helped disco attain a popularity with all ages not seen since *The Twist*, and once
again rock became predictable and acceptable.

As if in protest, the disenfranchised and disenchanted started the punk-rock movement,
refusing to dance their troubles away. From England came The Sex Pistols, The Clash and
Elvis Costello, while America contributed The Ramones, Blondie and Patti Smith. Though
the movement itself was short-lived, punk rock did bring outrage and rebellion back into
rock and roll. By the end of the 70s, this harder rock sound was being spread by such new
bands as The Cars, Talking Heads and The Police.

The diversity of the 70s music scene proved that rock and roll would never be one unifying
movement. Trends came and went more rapidly as the public's need for new sounds escalated.

In den 70er Jahren gelangte die ICH-Generation an die Macht, nachdem die WIR-Generation der 60er Jahre bedingungslos kapituliert hatte. Die Kriegskinder waren jetzt Anfang 30, und aus WIR wurden allmählich SIE. Die Musik einer Generation splitterte sich in unterschiedliche Genres auf, die eher Narzissmus als Idealismus widerspiegelten.

Der erste Trend in den 70er Jahren war die Auflösung erfolgreicher Gruppen der 60er Jahre. 1970 trennten sich die Beatles, um ihre Solokarrieren zu verfolgen. 1971 landeten Michael Jackson und Rod Stewart die ersten Hits ohne ihre Gruppen und reihten sich in die wachsende Zahl der Solostars wie Elton John, Billy Joel, Cat Stevens, James Taylor und Jim Croce ein. Sängerinnen wie Linda Ronstadt, Carly Simon, Carole King und Olivia Newton-John wurden Stars. Für alle, die ein abwechslungsreicheres Musikspektrum interessierte, hielten Led Zeppelin und Kiss den Heavy-Metal-Sound am Leben, während Marc Bolan, David Bowie und The New York Dolls den Glitter-Rock erfanden. Den progressiven Rock repräsentierten Yes, Roxy Music und Pink Floyd.

Der aufgesplitterten Rockszene der 70er Jahre entsprach in kommerzieller Hinsicht der Disco-Tanzfilm „Saturday Night Fever". Das Soundtrack-Album konnte gar nicht schnell genug produziert werden, so groß war die Nachfrage und mit 25 Millionen verkauften Exemplaren verzeichnete es bald einen beispiellosen Umsatz. Gloria Gaynor, The Village People und Donna Summer trugen dazu bei, dass die Disco-Musik bei allen Generationen einen Beliebtheitsgrad erreichte, wie es ihn seit dem Twist nicht mehr gegeben hatte, und Rock wurde erneut berechenbar und akzeptabel.

Aus Protest riefen die gesellschaftlichen Außenseiter und Desillusionierten, die sich weigerten, ihre Probleme „wegzutanzen", die Punk-Rock-Bewegung ins Leben. Aus England kamen The Sex Pistols, The Clash und Elvis Costello, während Amerika The Ramones, Blondie und Patti Smith beisteuerten. Der Bewegung selbst war zwar kein langes Leben beschieden, doch der Punk Rock brachte schockierende und rebellische Elemente zurück in den Rock 'n' Roll. Gegen Ende der 70er Jahre wurde dieser härtere Rock-Sound von neuen Bands wie The Cars, Talking Heads und The Police verbreitet.

Die Vielfalt der Musikszene der 70er Jahre machte deutlich, dass der Rock 'n' Roll nie wieder eine einheitliche Bewegung sein würde. Die Trends wechselten genauso schnell, wie das scheinbar unersättliche Publikum nach immer neuen Sounds verlangte.

Après la reddition inconditionnelle de la génération NOUS des années soixante, la génération MOI des années soixante-dix prit le pouvoir. A mesure que les enfants de la guerre abordaient la trentaine, NOUS devenions EUX. Le son d'une génération éclatait en divers genres musicaux qui reflétaient le narcissisme plutôt que l'idéalisme.

La première caractéristique des années soixante-dix parut être la désintégration des grands groupes des années soixante. En 1970, les Beatles se séparèrent pour entamer des carrières séparées. En 1971, Michael Jackson et Rod Stewart sortaient leurs premiers tubes solo, grossissant les rangs de stars solitaires comme Elton John, Billy Joel, Cat Stevens, James Taylor et Jim Croce. En outre, de nombreuses chanteuses comme Linda Ronstadt, Carly Simon, Carole King et Olivia Newton-John devinrent des stars à part entière. Pour ceux qui recherchaient des formes musicales plus variées, Led Zeppelin et Kiss continuaient sur la lancée du *heavy metal*, alors que Marc Bolan, David Bowie et les New York Dolls inventaient le *glitter rock*. La cohorte des musiciens de *progressive rock* était emmenée par Yes, Roxy Music, et Pink Floyd.

La sortie du film disco *Saturday Night Fever* (« La fièvre du samedi soir ») fédéra commercialement la scène rock éclatée des années soixante-dix. Le public dévalisa les disquaires et avec 25 millions d'exemplaires vendus, l'album devint le n°1 des musiques de film de tous les temps. Gloria Gaynor, les Village People et Donna Summer rendirent le disco populaire dans toutes les générations, performance sans exemple depuis le twist, et le rock redevint prévisible et acceptable.

Comme en signe de protestation, marginaux et désenchantés lançaient le mouvement punk, refusant d'évacuer leurs problèmes dans la danse. D'Angleterre arrivèrent les Sex

Pistols, les Clash et Elvis Costello, tandis que l'Amérique engendrait les Ramones, Blondie et Patti Smith. Tout éphémère qu'il fut, le mouvement punk réintroduisit néanmoins outrance et révolte dans le rock'n'roll. A la fin des années soixante-dix, de nouveaux groupes comme les Cars, Talking Heads et Police popularisaient ce son plus dur.

La diversité de la scène musicale des années soixante-dix prouva que l'unité du mouvement rock appartenait à un passé révolu. Les tendances apparaissaient et disparaissaient toujours plus vite et la soif du public pour des sons nouveaux paraissait inextinguible.

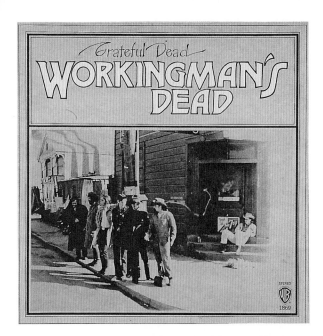

Grateful Dead
Workingman's Dead
Warner Bros., 1970

Design: Mouse Studios/
Toon N' Tree

Crosby, Stills, Nash & Young
Déjà vu
Atlantic, 1970

Design: Gary Burden
Photo: Tom Gundelfinger
Courtesy Atlantic Recording Corp.

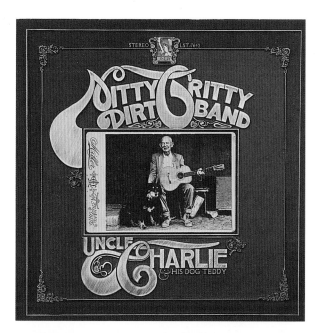

Nitty Gritty Dirt Band
Uncle Charlie & His Dog Teddy
Liberty, 1970

Design: Dean O. Torrance/
Kittyhawk Graphics Executive Art

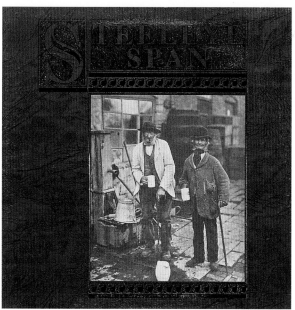

Steeleye Span
*Then Man Mop Or Mr. Reservoir
Butler Rides Again*
Pegasus, 1971

Design: Unknown

Procol Harum
A Salty Dog
A&M, 1969

Design: Dickinson

Joe Walsh
The Smoker You Drink The Player You Get
Dunhill, 1973

Design: Jimmy Wachtel

The Sutherland Bros. & Quiver
Lifeboat
Island, 1973

Design: Barney Bubbles/C.C.S.

Jethro Tull
Aqualung
Reprise, 1971

Painting: Burton Silverman

Led Zeppelin
Led Zeppelin
Atlantic, 1969

Design: Graphreaks
Illustration: "The Hermit" by
Barrington Colby, MOM
Courtesy Atlantic Recording Corp.

Genesis
Nursery Cryme
Buddah, 1971

Design: Unknown

Supercharge
Supercharge
Virgin, 1976

Design: Ed Lee
Photo: Eric Meola

Ry Cooder
Into The Purple Valley
Reprise, 1972

Art Direction: Ed Thrasher
Photo: Marty Evans

Chris Spedding
Chris Spedding
Rak/EMI, 1976

Design: Gered Mankowitz
(Tinting by Arthur Allen)

Neil Young
On The Beach
Reprise, 1974

Design: Gary Burden
for R. Twerk & Co.
Photo: Bob Seidemann

Leon Redbone
On The Track
Warner Bros., 1975

Design: Chuck Jones

The Kinks
Schoolboys In Disgrace
RCA, 1975

Art Direction: Chris Hopper
Illustration: Mickey Finn

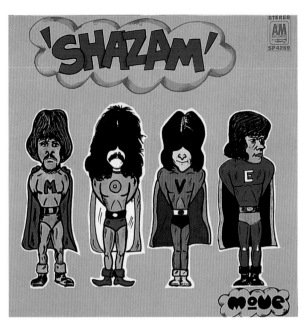

Move
Shazam
A&M, 1969

Design: Nickleby

Jefferson Airplane
Thirty Seconds Over Winterland
Grunt, 1973

Design: Bruce Steinberg

Phil Ochs
Gunfight At Carnegie Hall
A&M, 1975

Art Direction: Mike Yazzolino
Cover Art: Larry Hall

The Manhattan Transfer
Jukin'
Capitol, 1971

Design: Curtis Gathje

Montrose
Warner Bros. Presents 'Montrose'!
Warner Bros., 1975

Illustration: Harry Rossit

Judi Pulver
Pulver Rising
MGM, 1973

Design: Jimmy Watchell/S. Botticelli
Photo: Lorrie Sullivan/Jimmy Watchtell

Melissa Manchester
For The Working Girl
Arista, 1980

Design: Ria Lewerke-Shapiro
Photo: George Hurrell

Golden Earring
Moontan
MCA, 1974

Photo: Ronnie Hertz

off the record

Sweet
Off The Record
Capitol, 1977

Design: Norman Goodman
Artwork: Terry Pastor

Spinners
The Best Of Spinners
Atlantic, 1978

Art Direction: Bob Defrin
Illustration: David Williardson
Courtesy Atlantic Recording Corp.

Richard & Linda Thompson
Pour Down Like Silver
Island, 1975

Design: ABD Al-Lateef
Photo: ABD Al-Adheim

Marianne Faithfull
Broken English
Island, 1979

Photo: Dennis Morris

Nico
The Marble Index
Elektra, 1968

Design: Robert L. Heimell
Art Direction: William S. Harvey
Photo: Guy Webster
Courtesy Elektra Entertainment Group

Paul Simon
Paul Simon
Columbia, 1971

Design: Ron Coro/John Berg
Photos: P. A. Harper

Leo Kottke
My Feet Are Smiling
Capitol, 1973

Design: John Van Hamersveld
Photo: Norman Seef

Billy Joel
The Stranger
Columbia, 1977

Photo: Jim Houghton

Lou Reed
Coney Island Baby
RCA, 1976

Design: Mick Rock

Joe Jackson
Look Sharp!
A&M, 1979

Art Direction: Michael Ross
Photo: Brian Griffin

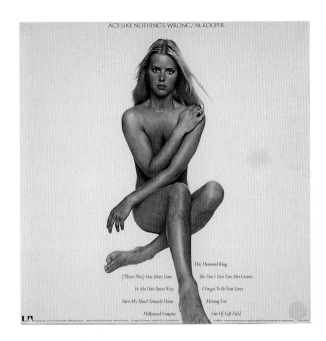

Al Kooper
Act Like Nothing's Wrong
United Artists, 1976

Design & Photo: Norman Seef
Concept: Al Kooper

(Back cover)
Act Like Nothing's Wrong

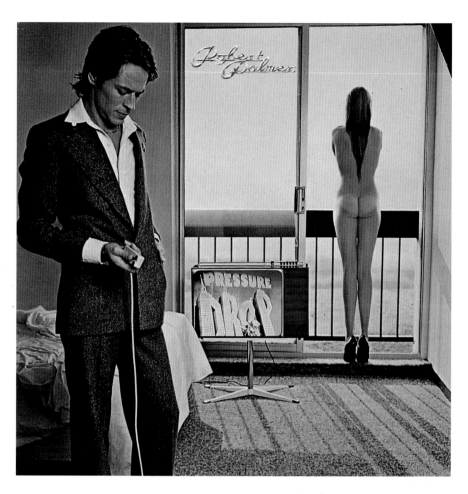

Robert Palmer
Pressure Drop
Island, 1975

Design: Graham Hughes

Rush
Hemispheres
Mercury, 1978

Art Direction:
Hugh Syme & Bob King
Graphics: Hugh Syme
Photo: Fin Costello

Average White Band
The Best Of Average White Band
RCA, 1979

Design: Laurence Hoadley
Photos: Duffy

Yes
Going For The One
Atlantic, 1977

Design: Hipgnosis
Courtesy Atlantic Recording Corp.

Deep Purple
Stormbringer
Warner Bros., 1974

Design: John Cabalka
Art Direction: Ed Thrasher
Illustration: Joe Garnett

Meat Loaf
Bat Out Of Hell
Epic, 1977

Design: Ed Lee
Concept: Jim Steinmen
Illustration: Richard Corben

The Graeme Edge Band Featuring Adrian Gurvitz
Kick Off Your Muddy Boots
Threshold, 1975

Design: Petagno III

Firefall
Firefall
Atlantic, 1976

Concept: Jock Bartley
Artwork: Ralph Wernli
Art Direction: Bob Defrin
Courtesy Atlantic Recording Corp

The Rolling Stones
Sticky Fingers
Rolling Stones, 1971

Design: Craig Braun, Inc.
Concept & Photo: Andy Warhol

The Rolling Stones
Some Girls
Rolling Stones, 1978

Design: Peter Corriston

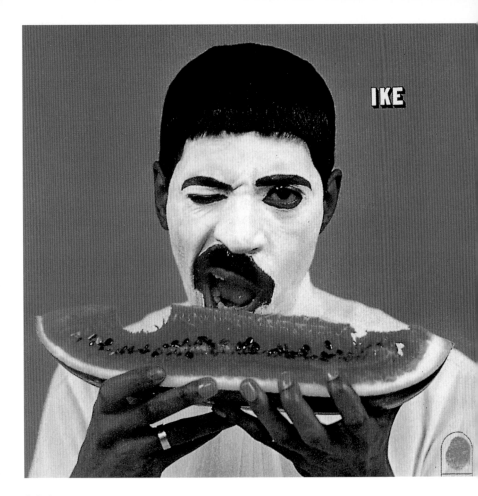

Ike & Tina Turner
Outta Season
Blue Thumb, 1969

Design & Photo: Amos & Andy

TINA

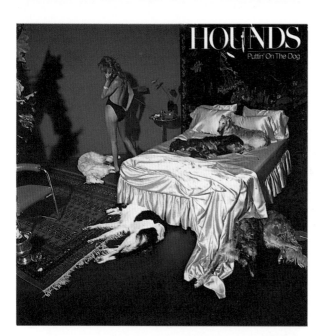

The Hounds
Puttin' On The Dog
Columbia, 1975

Photo: McGowan/Coder

Silverhead
16 And Savaged
MCA, 1973

Design: Chelita Secunda
Photo: Keith Morris

Sad Cafe
Fanx Ta–Ra
RCA, 1977

Design: Graves Aslett Associates,
Ltd., London
Concept: Carole Lisberg
Photo: Gered Mankowitz

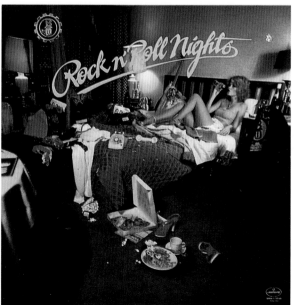

Bachman Turner Overdrive
Rock 'n' Roll Nights
Mercury, 1979

Concept: BTO
Art Direction & Photo:
James O'Mara

UFO
Force It
Chrysalis, 1975

Design: Hipgnosis

Godley & Creme
Freeze Frame
Polydor, 1979

Design: Hipgnosis

Foreigner
Head Games
Atlantic, 1979

Art Direction: Sandi Young
Photo: Chris Callis
Courtesy Atlantic Recording Corp.

Chris De Burgh
At The End Of A Perfect Day
A&M, 1977

Design: Nick Marshall
Art Direction: Fabio Nicoli
Photo: Roger Stowell

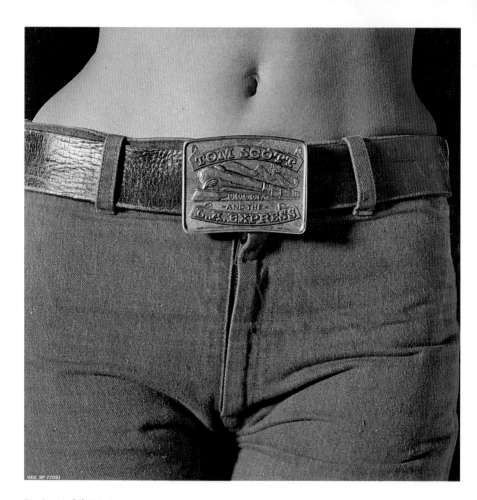

ODE SP 77021

Tom Scott And The L.A. Express
Tom Scott And The L.A. Express
A&M/Ode, 1974

Graphic Design: Chuck Beeson
Patch & Buckle: Joe Garnett
Photo: Jim McCrary

Adrian Gurvitz
The Way I Feel
Jet, 1979

Art Direction: Paul Welch/
Acrobat Design
Photo: Keith Ramsden

Love And Kisses
Love And Kisses
Casablanca, 1977

Photo: Alan Murano

Slade
Slayed?
Polydor, 1972

Photo: Gered Mankowitz

New York Dolls
New York Dolls
Mercury, 1973

Photo: Toshi

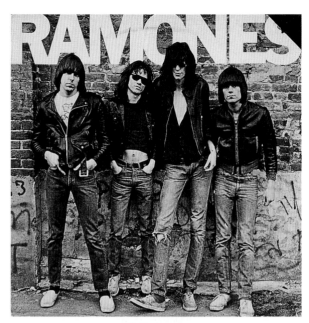

The Ramones
Ramones
Sire, 1976

Photo: Roberta Bayley
Courtesy Punk Magazine

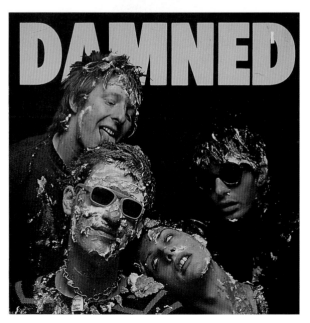

The Damned
Damned, Damned, Damned
Stiff, 1970s

Design: Big Jobs, Inc.
Courtesy Atlantic Recording Corp.

Loverboy
Get Lucky
Columbia, 1981

Design: John Berg
Photo: David Kennedy

The Marshall Tucker Band
Tuckerized
Warner Bros., 1982

Art Direction: Nancy Greenberg
Photo: Arnold Rosenberg

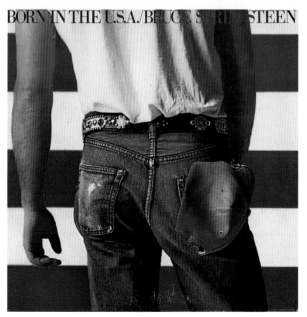

Bruce Springsteen
Born In The U.S.A.
Columbia, 1984

Design & Art Direction: Andrea Klein
Photo: Annie Leibovitz

1980s–90s

As the 80s began, rock and roll and its faithful followers had reached the second half of their lives. In *My Generation*, The Who sang the lyrics "I hope I die before I get old." Too many rockers lived and died by those lines. In the first three years of the 80s alone, John Lennon, Marvin Gaye, Bob Hite, Bob Marley, John Bonham and Dennis Wilson all died of unnatural causes. Yet rock music, rather then dying or fading away, became bigger than ever.

MTV, a total music cable station launched in 1981, brought music videos into homes 24 hours a day. Stars could now be made overnight and could just as easily become yesterday's news the following morning.

The business of music became a billion-dollar industry and needed more megastars to feed the new media machinery. Michael Jackson's *Thriller* album became the biggest selling album of all time, Madonna sold more records than any other female performer in history, and Whitney Houston had seven consecutive number-one hits. Many stars, including Diana Ross and Elton John, left the record companies that had established them for multi-million-dollar contracts with new labels, only to return to their original labels the same decade, much older, wiser – and richer. The Who, The Doobie Brothers, Yes, The Eagles and Steely Dan all disbanded only to reunite again for another payday.

Youthful music movements like rap and hip-hop tried to bring rock back downtown, but most of the multi-millionaire rock stars preferred to stay uptown. The rebellious punk-rock movement didn't lose its anger but became more musical, with new-wave acts like Graham Parker, Elvis Costello and The Clash. Garage-rock was transformed into grunge-rock with Nirvana and Pearl Jam.

Perhaps the single most important trend in pop music was the development in 1982 of the compact disc. CD sales had expanded enormously by the mid-eighties and by the end of the decade, the manufacture of vinyl record albums was virtually phased out. The record album became a relic of the past, and the room for cover art in this new format was reduced from twelve to five inches. The public gleefully discarded their record collections;

however, for the first time in rock history, almost everything that had been recorded previously was being preserved and reissued. There would be no last waltz.

Anfang der 8oer Jahre hatten der Rock 'n' Roll und seine treuen Anhänger die zweite Lebenshälfte erreicht. In ihrem Song *My Generation* sangen The Who „I hope I die before I get old". Viel zu viele Rockmusiker lebten und starben nach dieser Maxime. Allein zwischen 1980 und 1983 starben John Lennon, Marvin Gaye, Bob Hite, Bob Marley, John Bonham und Dennis Wilson eines unnatürlichen Todes. Aber die Rockmusik war weit davon entfernt, schwächer zu werden oder gar zu sterben, sondern wurde im Gegenteil bedeutender denn je.

1981 wurde der Musiksender MTV gestartet, der die Menschen zu Hause rund um die Uhr mit Musikvideos versorgte. Stars konnten nun über Nacht geboren werden und am nächsten Tag schon wieder Schnee von gestern sein.

Die Musikbranche wurde zu einem Milliardengeschäft und brauchte mehr Mega-Stars, um die neue Medienmaschinerie zu füttern. Michael Jacksons *Thriller*-Album wurde zum größten Verkaufsschlager aller Zeiten, Madonna verkaufte mehr Schallplatten als irgendeine andere Popsängerin in der Musikgeschichte und Whitney Houston landete hintereinander sieben Top-Hits. Viele Stars, darunter Diana Ross und Elton John, verließen ihre Plattenfirmen, die sie berühmt gemacht hatten, und schlossen mit neuen Labels Millionen-Dollar-Verträge ab, nur um noch im selben Jahrzehnt zu ihren ersten Plattenfirmen zurückzukehren – älter, klüger, reicher. The Who, The Doobie Brothers, Yes, The Eagles und Steely Dan lösten sich auf und taten sich dann wieder zusammen, um noch einmal das große Geld zu machen.

Junge Trends wie Rap und Hip Hop versuchten, den Rock zurück in die Innenstädte zu bringen, doch die meisten Rockstars, inzwischen Multimillionäre, blieben lieber in den vornehmen Villenvierteln. Die rebellische Punk-Rock-Bewegung war zwar zornig wie eh und je, wurde aber durch Vertreter des New Wave wie Graham Parker, Elvis Costello und The Clash musikalischer. Aus dem Garage Rock der Amateur- oder Garagenbands wurde der Grunge-Rock von Gruppen wie Nirvana und Pearl Jam.

Der größte und innovativste Schub für die Popmusik kam mit der Entwicklung der Compact Disc im Jahr 1982. Mitte der 80er Jahre hatte sich die CD auf dem Markt durchgesetzt und gegen Ende des Jahrzehnts wurde die Herstellung von Vinylschallplatten praktisch eingestellt. Nun gehörte auch die Langspielplatte der Vergangenheit an und die Fläche für die grafische Gestaltung der Cover reduzierte sich von 30 Zentimeter Durchmesser auf knapp 13 Zentimeter. Doch die Musikfreunde trennten sich leichten Herzens von ihren Plattensammlungen. Zum ersten Mal in der Geschichte der Rockmusik wurden sämtliche Aufnahmen der Vergangenheit neu eingespielt und auf den Markt gebracht. Einen letzten Walzer würde es nicht geben.

A l'aube des années quatre-vingt, le rock'n'roll et ses adeptes convaincus entamaient la seconde moitié de leur vie. *I hope I die before I get old* (« J'espère mourir avant d'être vieux ») chantaient les Who dans *My Generation*. Un vœu qui a fait des ravages chez les rockers : entre 1980 et 1983, John Lennon, Marvin Gaye, Bob Hite, Bob Marley, John Bonham et Dennis Wilson décédaient de mort non naturelle. Mais la musique rock, quant à elle, loin d'agoniser ou de disparaître, était plus florissante que jamais.

Lancée en 1981, la MTV, chaîne câblée entièrement musicale, enchaînait les clips vingt-quatre heures sur vingt-quatre. Fabriquées en une nuit, les stars pouvaient aussi bien disparaître du jour au lendemain.

Devenu une industrie milliardaire, le marché de la musique réclamait toujours plus de superstars pour nourrir la machinerie des nouveaux médias. L'album *Thriller* de Michael Jackson devint le disque le plus vendu de tous les temps. Madonna vendait plus de disques que n'importe quelle autre chanteuse dans l'histoire et Whitney Houston alignait sept n°1 consécutifs. De nombreuses stars, dont Diana Ross et Elton John, quittaient les maisons de disques qui les avaient lancées pour des contrats faramineux avec d'autres labels, pour revenir ensuite plus vieux, plus sages et plus riches vers leurs maisons d'origine. Les Who, les Doobie Brothers, Yes, les Eagles et Steely Dan se séparèrent, et se reformèrent ensuite pour des motifs financiers.

Des mouvements juvéniles comme le rap et le hip hop essayaient de ramener le rock au cœur de la ville, mais la plupart des rockstars multimilliardaires préféraient s'en tenir aux quartiers résidentiels. Le mouvement de révolte punk n'a pas renié sa colère mais il est devenu plus musical avec des musiciens *new wave* comme Graham Parker, Elvis Costello et les Clash. Avec Nirvana et Pearl Jam, le *garage rock* s'est transformé en *grunge rock*.

Le phénomène peut-être le plus important et le plus novateur de la musique pop fut la commercialisation du disque compact en 1982. Les ventes de CD augmentèrent considérablement au milieu des années quatre-vingt, et à la fin de la décennie, la fabrication de disques vinyle était pratiquement arrêtée. L'album 33 tours est devenu une relique du passé et l'espace graphique des pochettes ressemble à une peau de chagrin : on est passé d'un carré de 30 cm à un carré de 12 cm. Les gens ont allégrement bazardé leurs collections de microsillons. Pourtant, phénomène inédit dans l'histoire du rock, presque tout ce qui avait été enregistré a été numérisé et réédité : le rock n'a pas dit son dernier mot.

REO Speedwagon
Hi Infidelity
Epic, 1980

Design: Unknown

Manhattans
After Midnight
Columbia, 1980

Design: Paula Scher
Illustration: Mark Hess

Clocks
Clocks
Boulevard, 1982

Illustration: John Lykes

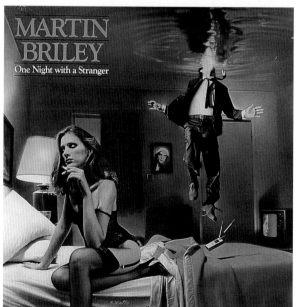

Martin Briley
One Night With A Stranger
Mercury, 1983

Design: Lumel Whiteman Studio
Art Direction: Bill Levy/
Murry Whiteman
Illustration: Stan Watts

It Bites
The Big Lad In The Windmill
Geffen, 1986

Concept: It Bites
Artwork: Stylorouge
Painting: David O'Connor

Paul Anka
The Painter
United Artists, 1976

Design & Art Direction: Ria Lewerke
Painting: Andy Warhol

Talking Heads
Speaking In Tongues
Sire, 1983

Design: Robert Rauschenberg

Judas Priest
Point Of Entry
Columbia, 1981

Design: John Berg
Photo: Art Kane

Simple Minds
Life In A Day
Virgin, 1987

Design: Unknown

Art In America
Art In America
Pavillion, 1983

Design: Ioannis

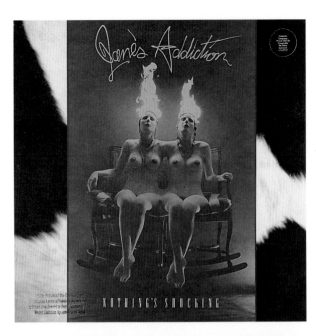

Jane's Addiction
Nothing's Shocking
Warner Bros., 1988

Design: Perry Farrell

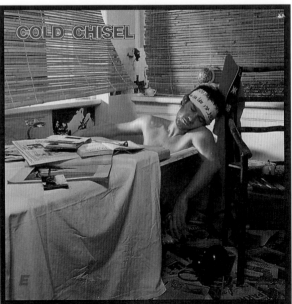

Cold Chisel
East
Elektra, 1980

Concept: Philip Mortlock/
Don Walker
Art Direction: Ken Smith
Photo: Greg Noakes

Marillion
Fugazi
Capitol, 1984

Design & Illustration:
Mark Wilkinson
Concept: Fish

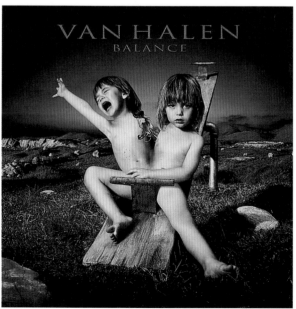

Van Halen
Balance
Warner Bros., 1995

Art Direction: Jeri Heiden
Photo: Glen Wexler

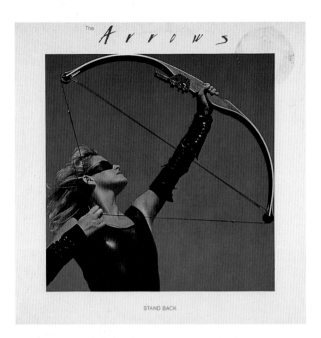

The Arrows
Stand Back
A&M, 1984

Art Direction: Dean Motter/
Diagram Studios
Photo: Patrick Harbron

Roxy Music
Flesh + Blood
Atco, 1980

Design: Bryan Ferry/Antony Price/
Neil Kirk/Simon Puxley/Peter Seville
Courtesy Atlantic Recording Corp.

10,000 Maniacs
In My Tribe
Elektra, 1987

Design: Kosh
Courtesy Elektra Entertainment Group

Heavy Pettin
Heavy Pettin
Polydor, 1983

Design: Gary Nichamin/
Boom Graphics
Concept: Al Kooper
Photo: Thom Elder

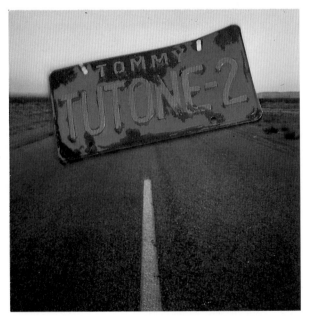

Tommy Tutone
Tommy Tutone-2
Columbia, 1981

Concept: Tony Lane, A.D./
Paul Cheslaw/David Gales
Photo: Bob Seidemann

Head East
U.S. 1
A&M, 1980

Design: Williardson & White Studios
Art Direction: Chuck Beeson
Illustration: Robert Bergendorff

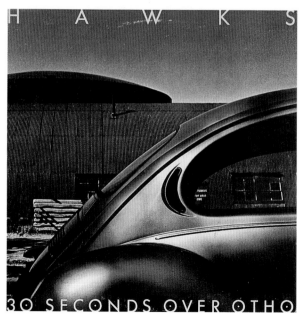

The Hawks
30 Seconds Over Otho
Columbia, 1982

Design: Andrea Kelin
Photo: Gary Jones

The Brains
The Brains
Mercury, 1980

Design & Art Direction:
Bob Heimall/AGI
Photo: John Paul Endress

A Flock Of Seagulls
Modern Love Is Automatic
Telecommunication
Jive, 1981

Design: Unknown

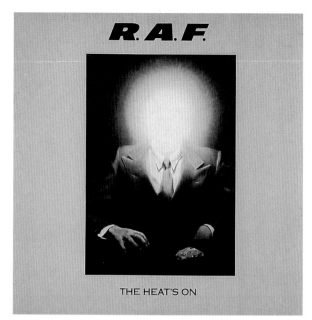

R.A.F.
The Heat's On
A&M, 1981

Art Direction: Michael Ross
Painting: "Le Principe du Plaiser"
by René Magritte, 1937

Pete Townshend
Empty Glass
Atco, 1980

Design: Bob Carlos Clarke
Courtesy Atlantic Recording Corp.

THE ONE THAT YOU LOVE

Air Supply

Air Supply
The One That You Love
Arista, 1981

Photo: G. Maxwell/Alpha

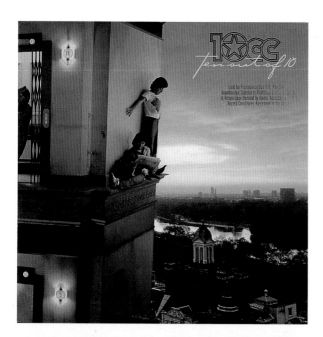

10 CC
Ten Out Of 10
Warner Bros., 1982

Design: Visible Ink, Ltd.
Photo: John Shaw

Harlequin
One False Move
Columbia, 1982

Design: Hugh Syme

Melissa Manchester
Mathematics
MCA, 1985

Design: Unknown

Diana Ross
Red Hot Rhythm + Blues
RCA, 1987

Design: Pietro Alfieri
Art Direction: Ria Lewerke
Photo: Herb Ritts

Pat Benatar
Crimes Of Passion
Chrysalis, 1980

Design: Unknown

Twisted Sister
Stay Hungry
Atlantic, 1984

Art Direction: Bob Defrin
Photo: Mark Weiss Studio
Courtesy Atlantic Recording Corp.

Ted Nugent
Scream Dream
Epic, 1980

Design & Art Direction:
Bob Heimall/Stephanie Zuraslagi
Photo: Lynn Goldsmith

Ozzy Osbourne
No Rest For The Wicked
CBS, 1988

Design: The Leisure Process
Photo: Bob Carlos Clarke

Blondie
Parallel Lines
Chrysalis, 1978

Design: Ramey Communications
Photo: Edo & Martin Goddard

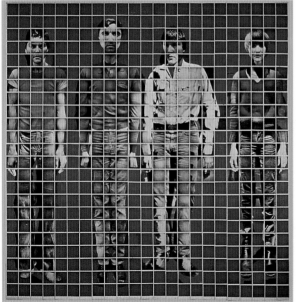

Talking Heads
More Songs About Buildings And Food
Sire, 1978

Concept: David Byrne
Reproduction: Jimmy DeSana

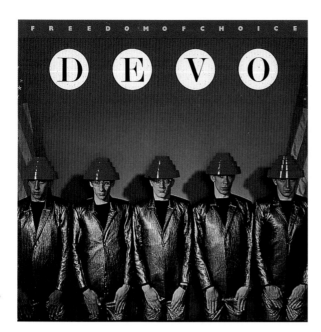

Devo
Freedom Of Choice
Warner Bros., 1980

Design: Artrouble

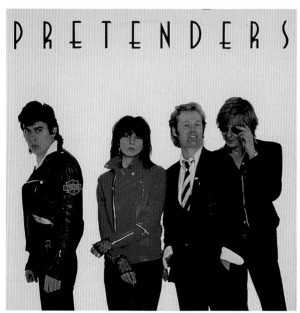

The Pretenders
Pretenders
Sire, 1980

Design: Kevin Hughes
Photo: Chalkie Davies

Laurie Anderson
Big Science
Warner Bros., 1982

Design: Cindy Brown
Art Direction: Perry Hoberman
Photo: Greg Shifrin

Peter Murphy
Deep
Beggar's Banquet, 1989

Design: Peter Murphy
Photo: Paul Cox

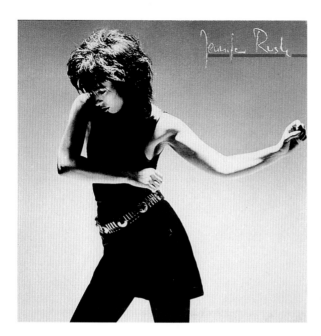

Jennifer Rush
Jennifer Rush
Epic, 1985

Design: Unknown

Bryan Adams
Cuts Like A Knife
A&M, 1983

Design: Lynn Robb & Mike Fink
Art Direction: Jeffrey Kent Ayeroff
Photo: Jim O'Mara

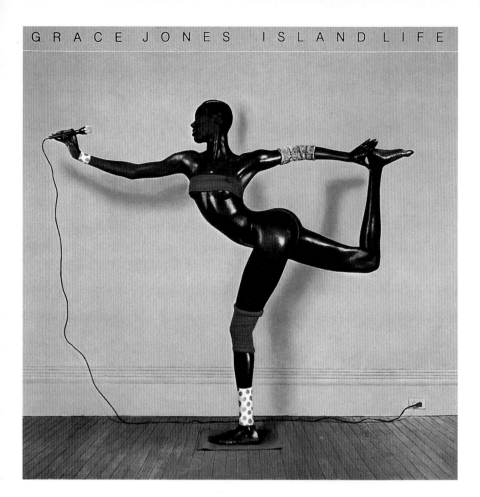

Grace Jones
Island Life
Island, 1986

Design: Greg Porto
Cover Art: Jean-Paul Gorde

Eurythmics
Touch
RCA, 1983

Design: Laurence Stevens/
Andrew Christian
Photo: Peter Ashworth

U2
The Joshua Tree
Island, 1987

Design: Steve Averill
Photo: Anton Corbijn

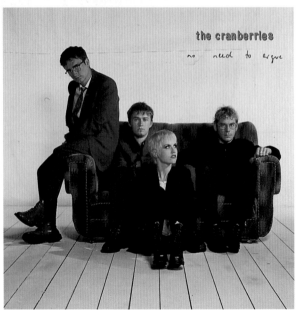

The Cranberries
No Need To Argue
Island, 1994

Design: Cally on Art DalkyIsland

Oasis
Definitely Maybe
Creation, 1994

Design: Brian Cannon for Microdot
Photo: Michael Specher Jonet

For more information Michael Ochs can be contacted at
Michael Ochs Archives
524 Victoria Avenue, Venice CA 90921, U.S.A.
www.michaelochsarchives.com

Michael Ochs developed an addiction to rock and roll in the early 50s. To feed his habit, Mr. Ochs headed the publicity departments of Columbia, Shelter and ABC Records in the 60s and 70s. He has also been a disc jockey, taught a rock-history course for UCLA and written for such magazines as *Rock, Melody Maker, Cashbox* and *Crawdaddy*. In the mid-70s, he established the Michael Ochs Archives in Venice (CA), which currently house millions of photographs and over 100,000 albums and singles. The majority of Rock books and CD reissues draws from these archives. *Classic Rock Covers* is Michael Ochs' sixth book.

Michael Ochs' Abhängigkeit vom Rock 'n' Roll datiert aus den frühen 50er Jahren. Um seine Sucht zu befriedigen, leitete er in den 60ern und 70ern die Presseabteilungen von Columbia, Shelter und ABC Records. Darüber hinaus war er Diskjockey, gab einen Kurs zur Geschichte der Rockmusik an der UCLA und schrieb für Zeitschriften wie *Rock, Melody Maker, Cashbox* und *Crawdaddy*. Die Firma Michael Ochs Archives gründete er Mitte der 70er. Es umfasst zurzeit einige Millionen Fotografien und mehr als 100.000 Alben und Singles. Fotos aus seinem Archiv finden sich in fast allen Büchern über die Rockmusik sowie auf unzähligen Wiederveröffentlichungen von Alben als CDs. Mit *Classic Rock Covers* hat Michael Ochs bereits sein sechstes Buch veröffentlicht.

Michael Ochs est devenu dépendant du rock'n'roll au début des années cinquante. Afin de satisfaire son irrépressible penchant, M. Ochs a dirigé le département publicitaire des maisons de disques Columbia, Shelter et ABC dans les années soixante et soixante-dix. Il a également été disc-jockey, a enseigné l'histoire du rock à UCLA et écrit pour des journaux et magazines tels que *Rock, Melody Maker, Cashbox* et *Crawdaddy*. M. Ochs a fondé les Michael Ochs Archives au milieu des années soixante-dix. Les Archives abritent aujourd'hui des millions de photographies et plus de 100.000 albums et singles. Des photos extraites de ces archives figurent dans la plupart des livres consacrés au rock et dans des rééditions d'albums en CD. *Classic Rock Covers* est le sixième livre de Michael Ochs.

Index

10CC 175
10,000 Maniacs 169

Bryan Adams 183
Air Supply 174
Steve Alaimo 69
Laurie Anderson 182
Paul Anka 163
The Arrows 168
Art In America 165
Frankie Avalon 68
Average White Band 138

Bachman Turner Overdrive 147
LaVern Baker 41
Hank Ballard And The
    Midnighters 52
The Beach Boys 78
The Beatles 107
Pat Benatar 177
Chuck Berry 52
Blind Faith 108
Blondie 180
Mike Bloomfield & Al Kooper 102
Bob B. Soxx And The Blue Jeans
    83
The Brains 172
Martin Briley 161
James Brown 86–87
James Brown And His Famous
    Flames 51
Ruth Brown 40
Jerry Butler 88

Cadets 42
The Cadillacs 49
The Chantels 44–45
Ray Charles 58–59
Dee Clark 67, 88
Clocks 161
The Clovers 46
The Coasters 49
Cold Chisel 166

Judy Collins 81
The Contours 93
Ry Cooder 122
The Cranberries 186
The Crew Cuts 33
Crosby, Stills, Nash & Young 116

The Damned 153
Reverend Gary Davis 39
Bobby Day 66
Chris De Burgh 149
Deep Purple 140
Devo 181
The Dixie Cups 82
Bill Doggett 51
Fats Domino 54–55
Donovan 81
Bob Dylan 103

Eurythmics 185

Fabian 69
Marianne Faithfull 132
Firefall 141
The Flares 77
A Flock Of Seagulls 172
Eddie Floyd 104
Foreigner 149
The Four Aces 31
The Four Coins 30
The Four Lads 31
The Four Lovers 70
The Four Preps 79
Inez & Charlie Foxx 93
Bobby Freeman 76

Hen Gates And His Gaters 26
Genesis 121
Godley & Creme 148
Golden Earring 129
The Graeme Edge Band 141
Grateful Dead 116
Adrian Gurvitz 151

Bill Haley And His Comets 61
Harlequin 175
Dale Hawkins 62
The Hawks 171
Head East 171
Heavy Pettin 170
The Jimi Hendrix Experience
    110–111
Clarence Henry 89
Lightnin' Hopkins 38
The Hounds 146
Freddie Hughes 104

The Isley Brothers 65
It Bites 162

The Jacks 43
Joe Jackson 135
Jan & Dean 79
Jane's Addiction 166
Jefferson Airplane 125
Jethro Tull 120
Billy Joel 134
Little Willie John 50, 53
Buddy Johnson And His Orchestra
    41
Grace Jones 184
Judas Priest 164

The Kinks 124
Al Kooper 136
Leo Kottke 134

Frankie Laine 28
Dr. Timothy Leary 96
Led Zeppelin 120
Jerry Lee Lewis 61
Little Anthony & The Imperials
    48
Little Richard 55
Julie London 28
Love And Kisses 151
Loverboy 154

The Mama's And The Papa's
    94–95
Melissa Manchester 129, 176
The Manhattan Transfer 126
Manhattans 160
Marillion 167
The Marshall Tucker Band 155
The Marvelettes 91
The McGuire Sisters 30
Meat Loaf 140
The Steve Miller Band 99
Joni Mitchell 102
Moby Grape 101, 109
Montrose 127
The Moody Blues 100
The Moonglows 47
Move 125
Peter Murphy 182
New York City 106
New York Dolls 152
Nico 133
Nitty Gritty Dirt Band 117
Ted Nugent 178

Oasis 187
Phil Ochs 126
The Olympics 76
Ozzy Osbourne 179
Johnny Otis 65

Robert Palmer 137
The Paragons/The Jesters 36
The Penguins 46
Carl Perkins 60
The Platters 48
Elvis Presley 56–57
The Pretenders 181
Procol Harum 118
Judi Pulver 128
R.A.F. 173
The Ramones 153
Johnnie Ray 29
Red Hot Chili Peppers 106

Leon Redbone 124
Otis Redding 105
Jimmy Reed 39
Lou Reed 135
REO Speedwagon 160
The Robins 27
The Rolling Stones 142–143
The Ronettes 85
Diana Ross 176
Roxy Music 168
Rush 138
Jennifer Rush 183

Sad Cafe 147
Sam & Dave 105
Tom Scott And The L.A. Express 150
Shep & The Limelites 54
The Sherrys 85
The Shirelles 82, 84
Silverhead 146
The Simon Sisters 80
Paul Simon 133
Simple Minds 164
Slade 152
Huey Smith And His Clowns 64
The Spaniels 47
Chris Spedding 123
Spinners 131
Bruce Springsteen 155
Steeleye Span 117
Supercharge 122
The Sutherland Bros. & Quiver 119
Sweet 130

Talking Heads 163, 180
The Teddy Bears 71
Ten Years After 99
The Thirteenth Floor Elevators 97
Richard & Linda Thompson 132
Johnny Thunder 77
Pete Townshend 173
The Toys 84
Ike & Tina Turner 92, 144–145

Tommy Tutone 170
Twisted Sister 178

U2 186
UFO 148

Van Halen 167
Vanilla Fudge 98
Various Artists
    (Boppin'!) 37
Various Artists
    (Dance The Rock & Roll) 27
Various Artists
    (Herald The Beat) 35
Various Artists
    (Jamboree) 32
Various Artists
    ("Rock, Rock, Rock") 33
Various Artists
    ("Rock All Night!") 32
Various Artists
    (Rockin' Together) 34
Various Artists
    (Teenage Party) 34
Various Artists
    (Whoppers!) 37
Gene Vincent And The Blue Caps
    63

Joe Walsh 119
Mary Wells 90–91
Jackie Wilson 67

Yes 139
Neil Young 100, 123

The publishers and Michael Ochs would like to thank:

Mary Katherine Aldin, Helen Ashford, Brad Benedict, Bernd Czogalla, Art Fein, Ursula Fethke, Richard Foos, Jonathan Hyams, Gary Johnson, Wayne Johnson, Jim Kennedy, Volkmar Kramarz, Ria Lewerke, Kathrin Marquardt, Ted Myers, Michele Phillips, Allan Rinde, Rockaway Records, Laura Weintraub, and West Coast Photo Lab, without whose help this book would not have been possible.

In addition the publishers would like to thank the following record companies and license holders for their support:

ABKCO, ACE, Alligator, Alternative Tentacles, Apple, Arista, Atlantic, Attic, AVI-Excello, Bearsville, Beggar's Banquet, BMG Ariola, Bug Music, Capitol, Castle Communications, CEMA, Chancellor, Charly, Evan Cohen, Creation, Crescendo, Roger Dean, DE-LFI, Disques Vogue, Eastwest, Elektra, Elvis Presley Enterprises Inc., EMI, Everest, Greensleeves, Gusto, Highland Music, Intercord, IRS, Jamie, King, Leadclass, LEGRAND, Line Music, Masters International, MCA, Me Company, Megaforce, Mercury, Mooncrest, Mushroom, Yoko Ono, Original Sounds, Overland, Philles, President, PolyGram, Radioactive, RCA, John Reid Enterprises, Repertoire, Rhino, Gerald H. Sanders, Slash, Sony, Sun, TKO, Trojan, Vee-Jay, Virgin, Warner Bros., WEA, Zomba, Zyx.

Special thanks are due to all designers, illustrators, photographers, and painters, etc., not mentioned by name, whose work has made this book what it is.

"Buy them all and add some pleasure to your life."

Art Now
Eds. Burkhard Riemschneider,
Uta Grosenick

Art. The 15th Century
Rose-Marie and Rainer Hagen

Art. The 16th Century
Rose-Marie and Rainer Hagen

Atget's Paris
Ed. Hans Christian Adam

Best of Bizarre
Ed. Eric Kroll

Karl Blossfeldt
Ed. Hans Christian Adam

Chairs
Charlotte & Peter Fiell

Classic Rock Covers
Michael Ochs

Description of Egypt
Ed. Gilles Néret

Design of the 20th Century
Charlotte & Peter Fiell

Dessous
Lingerie as Erotic Weapon
Gilles Néret

Encyclopaedia Anatomica
Museo La Specola
Florence

Erotica 17th–18th Century
From Rembrandt to Fragonard
Gilles Néret

Erotica 19th Century
From Courbet to Gauguin
Gilles Néret

Erotica 20th Century, Vol. I
From Rodin to Picasso
Gilles Néret

Erotica 20th Century, Vol. II
From Dalí to Crumb
Gilles Néret

The Garden at Eichstätt
Basilius Besler

Indian Style
Ed. Angelika Taschen

London Style
Ed. Angelika Taschen

Male Nudes
David Leddick

Man Ray
Ed. Manfred Heiting

Native Americans
Edward S. Curtis
Ed. Hans Christian Adam

Paris-Hollywood.
Serge Jacques
Ed. Gilles Néret

20th Century Photography
Museum Ludwig Cologne

Pin-Ups
Ed. Burkhard Riemschneider

Giovanni Battista Piranesi
Luigi Ficacci

Redouté's Roses
Pierre-Joseph Redouté

Robots and Spaceships
Ed. Teruhisa Kitahara

Eric Stanton
Reunion in Ropes & Other Stories
Ed. Burkhard Riemschneider

Eric Stanton
The Sexorcist & Other Stories
Ed. Burkhard Riemschneider

Tattoos
Ed. Henk Schiffmacher

Edward Weston
Ed. Manfred Heiting

www.taschen.com

ICONS